The Actor's Scenebook

The Actor's Scenebook

• • • •

Scenes for Beginning Actors to Create

• • •

Mack Owen

San Diego State University

• • •

HarperCollins*CollegePublishers*

Acquisitions Editor: Daniel F. Pipp
Project Editor: Claire M. Caterer
Design Supervisor: Mary Archondes
Cover Design: Mary Archondes
Text Illustrations: Nick Reid
Cover Photo: Students in rehearsal at AMDA, The American Musical and Dramatic
Academy, 2109 Broadway, New York, NY 10023. Photo taken by Gregory Rubin.
Production Manager/Assistant: Willie Lane/Sunaina Sehwani
Compositor: ComCom Division of Haddon Craftsmen, Inc.
Printer and Binder: R. R. Donnelley & Sons Company
Cover Printer: The Lehigh Press, Inc.

The Actor's Scenebook

Library of Congress Cataloging-in-Publication Data
Owen, Mack.
    The actor's scenebook : scenes for beginning actors to create /
Mack Owen.
        p.   cm.
    ISBN 0-06-500145-1
    1. Acting. 2. Improvisation (Acting) 3. Dialogues. I. Title.
PN2080.O94 1993
792'.028—dc20   92-4793
                                                                          CIP

98 99 10 9 8

Contents

Section Three   FINDING RHYTHM: PACE
AND RATE   121

To the Instructor

Here is a book of tools.

Teachers of beginning acting often find it difficult to find scenes that will help their students with specific problems. Classroom lectures, demonstrations, and exercises can fully illustrate the various areas students must explore, but when it's time for the new actors to get up on their feet, relate to one another in an active way, and begin the process of present-tense acting, the choice of material for working on these practical and individual tasks is severely limited.

So where are the tools the teacher can use to work on specific problems?

Here. This book contains forty scenes, each written with an individual specific acting problem in mind. Those in Section One are confrontations between characters in which a large amount of emotional energy must be developed and expended to get from the beginning to the end of the scene. The collection of scenes in Section Two gives the students textual and subtextual information for the building of effective characterizations. Since these scenes are not truncated snippets from larger, often very difficult works, the process is entirely self-contained and the problems are built into the dialogue—and no one has to compete with (or unconsciously duplicate) a vague memory of Vivien Leigh or Marlon Brando in *A Streetcar Named Desire*. Finally, the scenes in Section Three are built on a variety of problems in pace, rate, and build. The dialogue in these scenes is sometimes fast, sometimes slow; the transitions are sometimes gradual, sometimes sudden, in all possible combinations.

As an acting teacher who could not find such tools anywhere else, I wrote these scenes to solve the problems my students encounter most frequently, and also to fit easily into any beginning or intermediate acting class. There are no stage directions from previous productions and no memory of famous performances, so the student must build character and solve problems only from the real source of characterization: the words the character speaks and the actions the character performs. The teacher can assign the scenes to any combination of genders since no character names and no gender pronouns are used in the book. The scenes are compact: each gives the student enough time to solve the built-in problems, but not enough time for self-indulgence.

Then, too, a hidden bonus emerges as students work on these scenes. Because there is only dialogue, all other elements must be provided by the beginning actors, who must clothe these scenes in a history and environment unique to them. The muscles of imagination have been known to grow rapidly and enormously as they are exercised in these scenes.

So here is a book of specific tools for specific acting problems. I hope they are the right tools for you and that they prove as useful in your classroom as they have been in mine.

ACKNOWLEDGMENTS
• •

I would like to acknowledge those teachers other than myself who have already used these scenes in their classes, and whose response to them has been positive and most helpful: Christina Courtenay, Broderick Graves, Steve Gallion, Martin Katz, Robert Chapel, John Phillips, and William Anton.

I would also like to thank those people who read this book in manuscript and made useful comments: Bud Beyer of Northwestern University; Dorothy Corvinus of the University of North Carolina at Chapel Hill; Robert Funk, of the University of Alabama at Birmingham; Stephen Gerald, of the University of Texas at Austin; Bill Harbin of Louisiana State University; and Kennis Wessel of the University of Kansas.

Much gratitude is due the hardworking and patient people at HarperCollins: Melissa Rosati, Dan Pipp, Judith Anderson, and Claire Caterer, all of whom have been so valuable to me in the development of this book.

And most important are the people without whom this book would not exist, and to whom this book is gratefully dedicated: each and every one of my beginning and intermediate acting students who have displayed such extraordinary creativity and imagination in working on these scenes over the past few years.

—Mack Owen

To the Student

Think of this book as a kind of coloring book for actors. In these pages you will find the words that form the outlines of confrontation, characterization, and rhythm; the job for you, the student actor, is to fill in these linguistic outlines with your own choices of color and texture. As long as you stay more or less within the lines, you can bear down as hard as you like with dark, dramatic, theatrical shades or gently brush in more subtle and delicate tints of emotion; you can choose the vivid, theatrical colors of rage or hate, or you can select the pale, hinted-at pastels of indifference or affection. The choice is yours: you hold the crayon box.

The Actor's Scenebook presents the textual framework of a scene—the dialogue—and nothing else. There are no character names, no character descriptions, no stage directions from previous productions, no author's indications of pauses or emphasis, no director's notes on "pacing" or "builds." You will have to base your characterization on the spoken word—character dialogue—alone. The scenes even leave the choice of the sex of the characters open; no gender pronouns or titles are used, so anyone can work on any of the characters.

The scenes are short. Because each scene deals with one or two specific acting problems, there is no need for the lengthy devices of plot or complicated exposition. It is possible, then, to work on several of the scenes and the problems they contain in one semester. Two-person scenes are approximately three minutes long, and three-person scenes—you may be in a class with an odd number of students—are nearly five minutes in length.

The scenes are divided into three major sections, each of which provides exercise in an area frequently worked on in an acting class like yours:

1. Confrontations
2. Character constructions
3. Finding rhythm: pace and rate

Of course, some crossover occurs from scene to scene: every scene contains all of these problems to some extent; the focus in each section, however, is as indicated. What, exactly, do these categories mean?

The **confrontation scenes** are concerned with what seems to be the basis of almost all dramatic tension: human conflict between two or more characters. The problem you must solve in these scenes is to discover the way in which the argument or discussion or out-and-out fight develops, peaks, and resolves. How is the conflict introduced? Does it build directly, in a straight line? Or does the pattern curve and oscillate and jump irrationally around— as tends to be the case with most of our conflicts—with peaks being reached, then abandoned, then begun again from a new level or perspective? You might discover, for instance, that the confrontation involves "topping," each character using just a bit more intensity than the previous speech contained. Or a scene might show one character gathering strength while another lags behind. Does a scene involve a rapid-fire quarrel involving "dovetailed" or "telescoped" dialogue, in which each character begins to speak before the preceding line is finished, or do the characters wait their turn to lecture or harangue each other in longer speeches? When is the emotional peak reached in a scene? Do the characters peak at the same time or different times? How long is the peak or climax maintained? How is it resolved? Is more than one issue at stake? The scenes in the first section provide many opportunities to work on all of these aspects of confrontation, plus many, many more that you'll find on your own.

Character-construction scenes will give you the chance to create recognizable, fully dimensional human beings from nothing but the words they speak. The scenes will provide you with a multitude of clues as to what sort of person is speaking: the dialogue itself gives information about age, geographic location and regional orientation, education level, speech rate and fluency level, movement and gesture characteristics and limitations, mannerisms and eccentricities, as well as questions of intellect and temperament, fluidity and consistency of thought, and emotional coloration. You will provide your own biographical information and personality quirks, of course, to flesh out the ones suggested in the text. Just as when you're working in a fully produced play, you'll find that the sources of characterization are many and varied.

Constructing a character is arguably the greatest joy in the job of acting. Certainly it is the task that relates in the most personal, intimate manner to the actor, since the actor's personality and that of the character inhabit the same body. Here you are given the opportunity to work on a character unhampered by the luggage of previous performances from other actors. Go at this pleasurable creative task with imagination, integrity, and vigor. Of course, you must be sure the text supports all of your character choices; if it does, proceed to create freely and lavishly.

The third group of scenes will give you a good deal of exercise in discovering the rhythm of the scene and the words, phrases, and sentences that compose it. Careful, though: here you'll have to find the rhythm with no guideposts whatsoever. No pauses are indicated. No words are underlined to indicate stress or emphasis. No author's hints of "faster" or "slower" or "with increasing tension" are given. You must find the necessary silences, the rapid bursts of speech, the "telescoped," contracted line; the line that is continued past another character's speech; the interrupted phrase; the long, ambling—perhaps confused or intricate—speech. These scenes contain all these pace and rate variations, as well as many other rhythms that you will be able to determine from the length of the line, the context and environment that you create, the rhythm your partner establishes, and many other variables. You'll find out that the same scene can be done with different actors using different rhythms and be equally effective.

You will also have to make the decision as to whether or not an incomplete line is unfinished because it is interrupted by the next line or because the speaker cannot or will not complete the thought. And here you will find one small, but still ambiguous, punctuational hint given: the ellipsis (. . .) is used all the way through the book to indicate fragmented speech of all kinds. This punctuation will at least let you know that the speech is incomplete, but you'll have to decide why. In all cases, you'll have to find the rhythm of the scene from language, which is where it mostly comes from in everyday life.

There are not, of course, single answers to any of these problems. The words people choose—whether in a play or in reality—are always open to interpretation. Indeed, the subjectivity of speech has been known to cause more than conflict or misunderstanding. And often interpretations will vary widely from person to person—actor to actor. So the scenes may be duplicated in one classroom and still presented in many diverse ways, depending on the choices made by different actors. As a student, you may be fascinated by another team's completely different interpretation of the same scene. Your teachers may be surprised by the creativity and imagination the scenes stimulate in the class as a whole. And remember, the problems of confrontation, characterization, and rhythm—as well as many other acting challenges—exist in *all* of the scenes, not just those devoted to individual problems.

And don't neglect the direct challenge of these scenes to thoroughly research a character's life. Let the lines stimulate you to find out more about your character from many other sources. You'll have to do this when you're in a full play, so go ahead and start now. Then, too, there is the fascinating task of adapting a character's words to your own personality. Whether the character is completely different from you, very similar to you, or so unusual that he or she is like no one on earth, that character must inhabit the body of the actor. You'll have to find it in yourself to speak all the lines in this book *from* the character and *through* yourself.

So you're on your own with the words of the scenes and your box of crayons and vivid imagination.

Well . . . there is some help. At the beginning of each scene is a short guide to some of the problems you might encounter in the dialogue: some of the emotional and intellectual values to be searched for, some of the built-in technical problems, some of the tricks and traps that might lurk there. But plenty of secrets are not hinted at in the introductions. Look for them carefully; some of them will be more subtle, more difficult to find than others. Explore and research the scenes with the cold eye of reason; write a clear and logical character analysis; then revel in the creation of a new human being.

The Actor's Scenebook is meant to be used as a supplement to a complete methods text in your beginning or intermediate acting class, so it is presumed that your text and your instructor will have provided you with a basic actor's vocabulary. Following the scenes, however, is a glossary of the terms used in this preface and in the short introductions to the scenes themselves, just in case there are some you're not familiar with. The terms in this glossary are defined as the author understands them. For easy reference, those used for the first time in the introductions to the scenes are set in boldfaced type.

Color in the bare outlines with a lot of hard work, a good deal of fun, plenty of creativity, some essential integrity, and all the energy you've got.

Good coloring!

—M. O.

SECTION ONE

• • • •

CONFRONTATIONS

Drama is based on **conflict**, and actors relish a scene in which they can raise their voices in anger or their fists in combat. An **obstacle** that another character introduces often produces such a conflict, but the mere fact that one character confronts another with a differing opinion, a strong emotion, or a slap in the face does not mean you can simply let go with a barrage of emotional noise. No, the real tasks are finding the source of the confrontation within the text, understanding that source, supporting it with emotional truth, and pacing the attack so the audience does not tire too quickly of the very "sound and fury" of the scene. In every confrontation, there are basic questions to be asked: *Who* is your character? *Why* is he or she so angry or grief-stricken or fearful? *Where* does the emotion change? *How* are these changes shown in your voice and body? *When* does the scene reach a **peak**? *What* happens after that? Find these answers before you let yourself fall headlong into the emotion of the confrontation scene.

---   • • •   ---

Scenes for Two Actors

Scene 1

• •

The two characters in this scene seem to know each other, but do they both live in the "home" indicated in the first line? Does *either* of them live there? Do they both start out angry or tense? Why? Does anger derive from some real or imagined offense or from completely outside sources? Watch for sections that could be built by direct **topping**. How does **rate** differ in the longer speeches as opposed to the shorter, alternating dialogue? What is the event or action that happens—apparently out of the blue—that resolves, or at least tempers, the argument? Remember to stress words that need to be emphasized.

A: Anybody home?

B: Who is it?

A: Oh, hi. Me.

B: Who?

A: Me.

B: Oh. Hi.

A: Could you . . .

B: Just a minute.

A: Well, I've got these packages . . .

B: I'll be right there.

A: Okay, but . . .

B: What are you doing with all those packages?

A: Could you just unhook the screen door?

B: Sure.

A: Thanks.

B: Watch out!

A: Oh, for . . .

B: Sorry.

A: No problem.

B: Here, let me help you.

A: I can manage.

B: No, no. I insist.

A: I can manage.

B: No need to bite my head off.

A: Don't start with me!

B: What are you talking about?

A: Just leave me alone.

B: Fine!

A: Have you got any idea how annoying you can be sometimes?

B: Me? I'm annoying?

A: Yes! Yes, yes, yes, yes, yes!

B: You have got a hell of a nerve.

A: Oh, shut up! Just shut up!

B: No, I will not shut up! You come in here and start bossing me around before you even get in the door and I haven't done anything! Who do you think you are? I am sick of it. You hear me? I have had it! Just get out. Get out of here! Now!

A: No! I told you to shut up, and I meant it! Now shut up!

B: Put that down . . .

A: Why should I?

B: Please . . .

A: Oh, it's "please," now, is it?

B: I didn't mean . . .

A: Didn't you? Didn't mean what?

B: I didn't mean that you should get out. I just . . .

A: Sounded like you meant it to me. Sounded pretty definite to me.

B: No, no. I was just . . . I'm sorry. I really am.

A: Yeah, me too. I'm sorry I ever came here in the first place. I'm sorry I ever laid eyes on you. I'm sorry I didn't have sense enough to back off when things got too complicated. And most of all, I'm sorry you were ever born.

B: Now, listen . . .

A: But maybe we can do something about that, huh? Maybe we can fix it so you don't make anybody else's life as miserable as you've made mine. What do you think? You think that's a good idea? No, no, don't bother to thank me. It's my pleasure, believe me. Believe me!

B: I said I was sorry.

A: Not good enough.

B: What can I do to . . .

A: Nothing, absolutely nothing.

B: Please!

A: No!

B: Please!

A: No! Shut up!

B: Don't!

A: Yes!

B: Oh . . .

A: See? There's a solution to every problem.

SCENE 2

• •

Since the **environment** seems to be important to the **action**, the first thing to decide when you start work on this scene is where it takes place. That decided, the principal issue is one of focus: Who's listening to whom? Or not? And if not, why not? What are the techniques of switching focus from one thing or person to another? Watch for difficult **transitions**, especially the major one that forces a previously talkative character into responding in **subverbal** grunts.

A: I remember when there used to be a big oak tree over there . . .

B: Hmmm?

A: Strange place for an oak tree, I always thought, but then, when you think about it, not so strange after all, maybe.

B: Mmmm.

A: I mean, there're stranger places, I suppose. For an oak tree. You know what I mean? Anyway, I used to lie here and look at that tree and wonder how old it was. Oak trees can be really old, you know, and this was a big one, so I figured it was a hundred years old. Or more. And I always tried to picture what this whole place looked like when it was just a little twig. Maybe there was a whole grove of oak trees, a whole forest. Maybe there were all kinds of animals. There could have been rabbits and . . . and deer, maybe. Foxes. Maybe there were wolves. Sure, if it was more than a hundred years ago there could have been wolves. And birds, of course. All kinds of birds. Must have been nice, huh? Huh?

B: Mmm-hmm.

A: You haven't heard a word I've said, have you?

B: Mmm.

A: You don't hear a word I say, do you?

B: Huh?

A: You still don't. You're still not listening.

B: Hmm.

A: Hey!

B: What?

A: Finally.

B: You scared me to death.

A: Oh, did I?

B: Yes, you did.

A: Sorry to disturb your nap.

B: I wasn't sleeping.

A: Oh? Are you sure?

B: Of course I wasn't sleeping. I was . . .

A: You might as well have been.

B: What's that supposed to mean?

A: You're so self-involved.

B: I was just . . .

A: All you think of is yourself.

B: What is the matter with you?

A: I don't want to talk about it.

B: Oh, here we go again.

A: No, no.

B: I can't believe this. Never in my life have I seen somebody with mood swings like yours. I really think you should see a therapist or something, you know?

A: Right.

B: I mean, I never know where I am with you. I can be minding my own business, completely innocent, and all of a sudden I'm in the middle of a fight. It's crazy, you know? I mean, what's going on? Can you even tell me? Do you even know?

A: Huh?

B: Oh, and now you're going to have hurt feelings, are you? Going to just clam up and sulk? Is that it? You know, you really have a problem here. Did it ever occur to you that you need an awful lot of attention? Do you realize that you demand a lot from the people around you? Are you aware of that? No, probably not. You're one of those people who has been spoiled all their lives and expects other people to support them in every possible way, but especially emotionally. Do you realize how much emotional support you need?

A: Hmmp.

B: I just don't think it's fair. I have always believed that one of the signs of maturity was a willingness to stand on your own two feet emotionally. Anybody who can't is just a child and has no business being with grownups. That's what I think. You hear me?

A: Mm-hmm.

B: As a matter of fact, I think I better leave. I think it's time for you to find out what it's like to be on your own and responsible for yourself. You've got to be strong. Like that oak tree over there. You realize how long it's been standing there? What storms it's had to weather? That's what you've got to be like, and the only way that'll happen is for you to be on your own. So I'm leaving. Good-bye. I said good-bye. Hey, have you heard a single word I've said? Have you? Hey . . .

SCENE 3

• •

The following two characters sound as though they know each other well, but do they really? Are they actually talking to each other or to themselves? Or to a silent third character? Does irritation build up because of inattention? What is the physical environment? Is it hot or cold? How is temperature demonstrated by the characters? How do *you* demonstrate it? How does **pace** differ in the longer speeches and in the short, one-line dialogue? Do you find a difficult transition? How do you motivate it? When a previous statement is contradicted, how do you find **motivation?** How do you determine the pronunciation and definition of a "created" word such as *Shikasta-ism?* Watch out for pauses . . .

A: Of course, I never expected anything else from him. He was always the stupidest person that ever walked the face of the earth, if you know what I mean, but when he came right out and said that he was quitting I didn't know what to think.

B: I never knew him, but his brother was one of my best friends. He was kind of strange too, you know? Listen, have you ever heard of Shikasta-ism? It's some weird religion based on somebody's novel. Anyway, he was into that.

A: Not that I don't think that everybody has a right to do whatever they want to, naturally. I do.

B: I think he was a minister or a priest or something for this religion. He believed the world was surrounded by layers or something. Energy levels, he called them.

A: But when he just walked out, I couldn't believe it.

B: I didn't understand any of it.

A: I couldn't either. I just couldn't.

B: No, I really didn't.

A: So, how you been?

B: Oh, fine.

A: Really hot, isn't it?

B: Sweltering.

A: Course, I guess that's why people come here.

B: The heat?

A: Yeah, I guess.

B: You really think so?

A: Sure, what else?

B: Oh, I don't know. The food . . .

A: Nah, the food's mediocre.

B: You think so?

A: Yeah. Music's nice, though.

B: What music? And why would anybody go anywhere for heat?

A: You haven't heard the music? It's great. And I didn't really mean heat. I meant the sun.

B: Oh, well, the sun . . .

A: I mean, it's really been cold.

B: You think so?

A: Don't you?

B: Not really. Like I said, I . . .

A: I've been freezing.

B: . . . maybe you should see a doctor.

A: Why?

B: To check out why your . . . thermostat is screwed up.

A: My thermostat?

B: Well, you know, why you've been so cold when it's been so hot.

A: But it hasn't been hot.

B: That's what I mean. See, before you said . . .

A: You know, there's an interesting condition in which people are absolutely unable to face facts. I forget what it's called, but that could be the root of your trouble. Maybe if you saw a therapist . . .

B: You could have a thyroid condition. I had an aunt who had that kind of trouble once. She turned to the left every time somebody said "turn right." And vice versa. Did everything backwards. She had a thyroid condition.

A: I think everybody needs therapy at some time in their lives.

B: I bet that's all you need: a good thyroid checkup.

A: Anyway, nice talking to you.

B: You, too. See you later.

A: Take it easy.

B: Right. By the way . . .

A: What was your name again?

SCENE 4

• •

What on earth are these people doing? And where? Or maybe it isn't on earth at all. Perhaps you, the actors, will have to create a whole new environment. How do you motivate all the nonsequiturs? How do you react to one? There's another neologism (*plegoit*) to find a pronunciation for. Was one character actually born on Mars? If not, is this a fantasy, a delusion, or a lie? What exactly is "B.C.E."? What happens at the end? In this scene, creativity and imagination are *very* important.

A: Marble statue of Zeus.

B: Check.

A: Seventh century B.C.E.

B: Check.

A: You about ready to quit?

B: You?

A: Just about.

B: One more.

A: Okay.

B: Then we'll quit.

A: Stack of magazines. Mostly *Mad* from the looks of it. Early sixties.

B: Check.

A: Lots of jellyfish.

B: Wonder what they're doing here?

A: No idea. Don't you know?

B: Nope. No idea.

A: Should we . . . ?

B: Nah, just leave them alone.

A: They'll be all right?

B: Oh, sure.

A: I've got to stop for a while.

B: Really?

A: Yes. I'm tired.

B: Well, sure, that's fine.

A: I'm going to sit down.

B: Why don't you pull over one of those elephants.

A: Is that what they are?

B: Oh, yes.

A: Gosh, I thought they were . . .

B: Ostriches?

A: . . . yeah.

B: No. They're elephants.

A: I wonder who sewed them like that?

B: No idea.

A: Somebody who's never seen an elephant, that's for sure.

B: No kidding.

A: You been here long?

B: Long as I can remember. Since before the war.

A: Really? Long time.

B: Seems like forever.

A: I just got here.

B: Yeah. I know.

A: Really? How?

B: You get tired too easy. Got to be new.

A: Oh.

B: You'll toughen up, though.

A: I certainly hope so.

B: Takes a while.

A: I'm sure.

B: Where you from?

A: Santa Barbara.

B: California.

A: Right. You?

B: I'm from Mars.

A: Really?

B: No, not really.

A: Oh, well, I'm disappointed. I've never met anybody from Mars.

B: Sorry.

A: Where are you really from?

B: Kenya.

A: Oh. That's how you knew about the elephants.

B: Right.

A: You been here so long, you know all about plegoits, too, I guess.

B: Sure.

A: Is it true they cut people's heads off?

B: Yep. As a matter of fact . . .

A: Oh! What's that you've got?

B: Plegoit knife.

A: Where on earth did you get it?

B: It's mine.

A: Oh . . . you mean, you're a . . . a . . .

B: A plegoit. Right.

A: Oh.

B: Want to see my knife?

A: Well . . .

B: Come on, take a closer look. Closer . . . closer . . .

SCENE 5

• •

Here the confrontation builds until one character explodes in a wordless scream. Where does all the tension come from? What sort of relationship do the two characters have? Or *did* have? Pauses are important in the **build** of the conflict; be sure to find them, and don't be afraid to make them as long as they need to be. One of these characters has the habit of speaking in clichés. How do you deliver such lines? Is the character aware that they are clichés? What difference is there in the delivery if the character is or is not aware? Examine the first line (and the next-to-last): Don't do what? Watch out for **interrupts**. Or are they incomplete sentences, that is, **trail-offs**? How do you tell the difference? How do you find your **cue** in each case?

A: Don't do that.

B: Sorry.

A: I said . . .

B: Sorry!

A: Honestly . . .

B: I said I'm sorry.

A: Sure.

B: If I asked you something, would you tell me the truth?

A: . . . yes.

B: First, swear that you'll tell the truth.

A: Don't . . .

B: That you'll be honest.

A: Look . . .

B: Really honest.

A: Yes!

B: Okay, then. Why are you acting like such a jerk?

A: Oh, God!

B: Now you're mad.

A: Give me a break . . .

B: I knew it.

A: I am not . . .

B: I knew you wouldn't be honest.

A: Shut up! You are driving me nuts.

B: I'm what?

A: You are . . .

B: I'm driving you nuts?

A: That's what I said.

B: I can't believe you said that.

A: Don't start.

B: I can't believe that after all this time and all this effort, trying to build a relationship, really trying to solve some problems, and you . . .

A: I said, don't start.

B: And you! You start bringing up this old . . .

A: Cut it out.

B: This old crap again. I mean, come on. You can't really expect me to sit quietly by while you go into a primordial tantrum, can you?

A: A primordial tantrum?

B: Let me tell you something. People don't do this. All people don't sit around pulling each other apart. They simply accept what other people do and think and say without analyzing every little word and deed. Do you know that? Huh? It happens to be true, so . . . don't look at me like that . . . so don't think you can get away with all that old . . . I said don't look at me like . . .

A: You know, you can be really strange.

B: I can? I can?

A: That's right.

B: I'm strange?

A: Yep.

B: Unbelievable.

A: But that's okay. I don't mind. It livens up my day. It keeps me from killing myself out of boredom. If you weren't so strange, I would have long ago given up on the vagaries of life and eaten my gun.

B: Eaten your . . .

A: Or jumped into the bay or entered a . . .

B: Okay, okay . . .

A: So don't ever let anyone criticize you for being weird. Your weirdness has saved my life.

B: Just cut it out, okay?

A: Well, isn't this what you wanted? A meaningful dialogue between the two of us?

B: All right, all right, all right, all right . . .

A: Interpersonal communication?

B: All right!

A: Causal oneness? Symbiotic activity? Between you and me?

B: Shut up!

A: Between you and the jerk?

B: Aaaaaaaahhhhhhh!

A: Okay?

B: Okay.

A: Don't do that.

B: Sorry.

SCENE 6

• •

This relationship is in trouble. Are these two close friends? Are they lovers? Who's lying to whom? How does the other know? Why do they care? Hint: One of the lies has to do with *Gone with the Wind.* Is one character a bad risk for loans? What are they looking at when the scene begins, and how does your answer to this question help define their environment? Find textual evidence for your answers to all of these questions or create answers. Find places for some long transitional pauses.

A: Look at that.

B: What?

A: That.

B: Good God.

A: Can you believe that?

B: No.

A: Me neither.

B: Incredible.

A: What do you think . . . ?

B: I don't know.

A: Oh, well. Takes all kinds, I guess.

B: I guess.

A: Where'd you go last night?

B: Me?

A: Yeah.

B: Oh. The movies.

A: The movies.

B: Hm?

A: The movies? That's where you were?

B: Yeah. The movies.

A: Oh. What'd you see?

B: . . . hm?

A: What did you see? What was on?

B: Oh. *Gone with the Wind.*

A: Really?

B: Yeah.

A: They released that again?

B: Yeah.

A: Great movie.

B: Yeah.

A: I love that part when Clark Gable gets killed, don't you?

B: Yeah.

A: And Vivien Leigh just stands there with that smoking gun?

B: Yeah.

A: Yeah.

B: What time is it?

A: Almost three o'clock.

B: Really?

A: Yeah.

B: I got to go.

A: Yeah.

B: Listen . . .

A: What?

B: Can you lend me a couple dollars?

A: Uh . . .

B: Say ten? Maybe even twenty?

A: Well . . .

B: Just till payday.

A: I'll tell you . . .

B: If it's a problem . . .

A: Well . . .

B: Don't bother.

A: I'll tell you what the problem is. One of them. Do you know what one of the problems is?

B: No. But you're going to tell me, I can see that.

A: Right. One of the problems is that you already owe me forty-five dollars.

B: What? I what?

A: You have owed me forty-five dollars since . . .

B: Come on . . .

A: For six months. For more than six months.

B: Forget it.

A: For almost ten months you've owed me money.

B: I said forget it.

A: No! I don't want to forget it. And more important, I don't want you to forget it.

B: What is this?

A: I want my money. I want . . . oh, so you're leaving, are you? Just walking out on the problem?

B: I'm sorry I opened my mouth.

A: You should be. Because every time you do, you tell a lie.

B: What?

A: You do. You lie and you borrow money and you don't pay it back.

B: I'm leaving.

A: Oh, go ahead.

B: You are hysterical. No, you're crazy.

A: Oh, right. I'm the crazy one.

B: I don't think you should've ever stopped therapy because you have obviously lost your mind and . . .

A: Get out!

B: Don't tell me what to do!

A: Get out!

B: Fine! I'm going! I'm out of here! Who wants to hang around with a crazy person?

A: Out!

B: And by the way, I wasn't at the movies last night!

A: I know that!

B: Oh, yeah? What are you doing, checking up on me?

A: No! But you are so stupid you didn't even know that in *Gone with the Wind* it isn't . . .

B: You're sick, you know that?

SCENE 7

• •

These two characters seem not to know each other at the beginning of the scene. Where are they? A bar seems almost too obvious a **choice**, but maybe it's the best one. Whatever choice is made, the construction of an environment by characterizational choices is very important. Are the "ghost" stories true or are they social maneuvers? How does this nonviolent confrontation go from tentative, casual conversation to a closer relationship? What different choices must you make to build effectively such a subtle confrontation? Remember that **filled pauses**—that is, pauses filled with thought—are important when two people are getting to know each other: they often indicate conversational switches and lapses of attention that are important in establishing the build of the relationship. Watch **subtext** choice on the last line; there are many different choices you can make.

A: Excuse me, do you mind if I . . .

B: Oh. No, not at all.

A: Thanks.

B: Sure.

A: Pretty hot.

B: Yes, it is.

A: And crowded.

B: Yeah.

A: Fun, though.

B: I guess.

A: You don't think so?

B: No, no. It is. I do.

A: I mean, I'm having a good time. Aren't you?

B: Yeah. I am. Sure.

A: Different from Seattle.

B: What?

A: I said it's different from this kind of place in Seattle.

B: Is it?

A: Yeah. It is.

B: How?

A: Oh, I don't know. It just . . .

B: More crowded?

A: Here?

B: Yeah. As opposed to Seattle.

A: Well, yeah. And hotter.

B: Uh-huh.

A: Nice, though.

B: You from Seattle?

A: No, actually, I'm from Portland, but I used to . . .

B: Oregon?

A: Huh?

B: Portland in Oregon?

A: Oh. Yeah.

B: As opposed to Maine.

A: Right.

B: And you used to . . .

A: What?

B: You started to say you used to . . .

A: Oh. Go up to Seattle a lot.

B: I see.

A: It's not far.

B: No.

A: I did live in Seattle for a little while though. I had this great apartment. Actually it was a loft. Right over a dry-cleaner place. It was on Queen Anne Hill and had a terrific view of the Sound. Real nice. Kind of noisy in the daytime, but not too bad.

B: Because of the dry cleaner?

A: What?

B: Noisy in the daytime because of the dry cleaner?

A: Yeah. That made it hot, too. From the steam. But in Seattle that was good, sometimes. You know, in the winter? Anyway, best thing about it was that it was haunted.

B: Get out.

A: No, it had a ghost. Really. I used to wake up in the middle of the night and I'd hear this little, tiny, high voice singing. Oh, yeah, it was haunted all right. Weird.

B: Singing what?

A: Huh? Oh. Well, it was different every night. Most of the time it was stuff from the sixties. Beatles songs, the Mammas and the Pappas, Simon and Garfunkel. That stuff. Kind of nice . . .

B: I'll bet.

A: Do you believe in . . .

B: Ghosts? Yeah. Yeah, I guess I do as a matter of fact.

A: Me too.

B: I guess so after that.

A: After what?

B: The . . . uh . . . your haunted apartment. Over the dry cleaner.

A: Oh. Yeah. Right.

B: Yeah.

A: Well . . .

B: I had a haunted car once.

A: A . . .

B: Car. A haunted 1972 Mercury Comet.

A: Like Christine?

B: What?

A: Christine. You know—Stephen King . . .

B: Oh. Oh, yeah. No. Not like that at all.

A: I see.

B: This was a nice haunting. Kind of like yours. Except no singing. No
noise, even. It just kept producing things.

A: Producing things?

B: Yeah. Every now and then I'd look in the back seat and there'd be
stuff there. A pencil or a handkerchief or a book or even a hat.
They'd just appear there one day. Nothing important. No big deal.
But there they'd be.

A: They weren't yours?

B: No. Oh, no.

A: Maybe they . . .

B: No. It was haunted all right.

A: I see.

B: I'd save the stuff for a while, then just toss it.

A: Huh.

B: Strange.

A: I'll say. Maybe we both attract them.

B: Attract what?

A: Ghosts.

B: Oh. Could be.

A: Yeah.

B: What's your name?

SCENE 8

• •

Establishing environment is important here. How does the choice of *what they're doing* affect *where they are*? And how does where they are affect things like **body stance**, **body gesture**, **hand/arm gesture**, and pace? Who is in control here? Is one lying at times? For instance, what *is* at 54 degrees north by 1 degree west? York? Why do you have to be certain of that? Why do they suddenly start talking about their childhoods? How do you make that transition? Are pauses useful in such a situation? What thoughts fill these pauses? Be imaginative when determining what the characters are watching for.

A: So I told him to cut it out and that was that.

B: No more problems?

A: Not a one.

B: Good.

A: About time, I'd say.

B: Uh-huh.

A: What a jerk.

B: I'll say.

A: Oh, well. Let's talk about something else.

B: Right.

A: Oh, look. Here comes one.

B: Where?

A: Over there.

B: I don't see . . .

A: Just behind the . . .

B: Oh, yeah. I see.

A: Good one.

B: Yeah, not bad. There it goes.

A: Yeah.

B: That makes twelve, right?

A: Thirteen, I think.

B: Really?

A: I think.

B: Hmm.

A: But I could be wrong.

B: Do you know anything about geography?

A: What do you mean?

B: Well, for instance, do you know . . .

A: I mean, I know what geography is, but . . .

B: . . . anything about longitude and latitude. Stuff like that?

A: Which?

B: Which what?

A: Which longitude? Which latitude?

B: Well, I don't know. I mean, I wasn't thinking about what's at 54 degrees latitude and 1 degree longitude or anything like . . .

A: York.

B: What?

A: York. In England. That's what's at 54 degrees north by 1 degree west.

B: . . . it is?

A: Yeah. Look it up.

B: . . . no, that's okay.

A: It's true.

B: Anyway . . .

A: It really is true. I know stuff like that.

B: Okay, okay. But what I really wanted to know was do you know about capitals and things like that?

A: Capitals?

B: Yeah. Like what's the capital of . . .

A: Peru? Lima.

B: No, no. The capital of . . .

A: Vermont? Montpelier.

B: Shut up. No. Listen.

A: Okay. Of what?

B: What I want to know is . . .

A: Look! Another one!

B: . . . oh, yeah. Good one.

A: Really!

B: Got the . . .

A: Yeah. Here.

B: Right.

A: Quick. Hurry.

B: Okay, okay . . .

A: It's going to . . .

B: I'm hurrying as fast as I can. There.

A: Got it?

B: Yeah.

A: Sure?

B: Yeah.

A: Fourteen.

B: Thirteen.

A: Whatever.

B: No, I'm sure.

A: When I was a little kid, I used to dream about going to the stars. Either the stars or Oz. I thought if I was very, very good that I'd go to Oz when I died. Or maybe I'd go to the stars or some real advanced civilization. You know what I mean?

B: I guess. For me it was rock groups.

A: What?

B: When I was a kid I wanted to be a rock star. You know, rich and famous. I didn't care what happened to anybody else. I just wanted to be rich and famous and a rock star.

A: Pretty self-centered.

B: Oh, I don't know.

A: Me, I just wanted to know everything.

B: Well, you made it. At least you think you did.

A: What kind of remark is that?

Scene 9
••

To a certain extent one of these characters is in control of the other. To *what* extent? Why? What is the object in the pocket and what does it do? Words are sometimes repeated in the scene, but obviously have a different effect the second time they're said. Why? How do you demonstrate authority vocally, physically? Subservience? In what locale do such relationships usually thrive? At what ages? If you choose to play the characters very youthfully, be sure to avoid **commenting (indicating)**. Be true and real.

A: What's that you've got?

B: Nothing.

A: What do you mean, nothing?

B: Nothing. Just nothing.

A: Don't be silly, now. Of course it's something.

B: No, it's not. It's not anything.

A: If you don't give it to me I'll . . .

B: What? You'll what?

A: Don't talk to me like that.

B: I will.

A: No, you won't.

B: Will.

A: No!

B: Okay. All right. Sorry.

A: You'll just never learn, will you?

B: It's not fair.

A: Life isn't.

B: Well, it could be.

A: Oh? How?

B: Well, you could start by not bossing me around so much.

A: I have your best interests at heart.

B: How do I know that?

A: You know I do.

B: No, I don't.

A: Oh, you're so ungrateful.

B: Why should I be . . .

A: If you would only stop and think how much better off you are now than you were a year ago, then you might be easier to get along with today. You know that you have come a long way in a year's time, and I don't see why being aware of that and showing a little gratitude is so difficult for you. Why is it?

B: I think you ought to thank me some time.

A: Right.

B: I do. Why don't you ever say thank you? I'm nice to you. I do things for you. All the time. Why don't you say thank you?

A: I do.

B: No, you don't. I gave you a book the other day and you didn't even say anything, let alone thank you. And I know I'm supposed to say thank you. You told me to and I do. But you never do.

A: Okay, I will from now on. From now on I'll say thank you.

B: Thank you.

A: Now, what have you got in your pocket?

B: Please.

A: Oh, for . . .

B: Please.

A: . . . please.

B: Thank you.

A: What have you got in your pocket, please?

B: This.

A: Where on earth did you get that?

B: I found it.

A: Where?

B: Just somewhere.

A: Where?

B: Well . . . in your room.

A: Yes. Of course you did. Now give it to me.

B: It belongs to me now.

A: No. It does not. It belongs to me.

B: I found it.

A: Yes. But in my room.

B: Yes.

A: So it's mine. Now give it to me.

B: No.

A: Now!

B: No!

A: Then I'll take it away from you.

B: No!

A: Yes!

B: That hurt.

A: Next time do what I tell you.

B: Why should I?

A: Now this is broken.

B: Your fault.

A: Your fault for taking it in the first place.

B: Always my fault.

A: In this case.

B: Always.

A: There. I fixed it.

B: What is it, anyway?

A: Well, if you must know, it does this . . .

B: Oh!

SCENE 10

••

The two characters in this scene talk about being in love. Are they in love with each other or with other people? What kinds of situations and environments bring out what are apparently irrational tensions? Or are these rationally motivated? Pauses are very important in this scene. In some cases there are rather long pauses within a line that will help you with delivery. Remember that the subtext for apparently illogical language must be as firmly based in subtextual reality and consistency as rational language is.

A: I've never been in love before.

B: Are you now?

A: Yes.

B: How do you know?

A: I can't explain it . . .

B: Oh.

A: Can you?

B: Explain about being in love?

A: Yes.

B: I could.

A: Then . . .

B: But I'm not going to.

A: Why not?

B: It makes me shy.

A: Yes, I can understand that.

B: I think it's one of those things that one just doesn't talk about.

A: Yes. What's another one?

B: Another one?

A: Thing that one doesn't talk about.

B: Oh, well . . . religion and politics.

A: But those are very interesting things to talk about.

B: Maybe, but they're disruptive.

A: No, not necessarily.

B: Oh, yes.

A: You really are sure of yourself, aren't you?

B: No, I just . . .

A: Oh, you are. You are. I mean, where do you get these rules and regulations, anyway? Are they written down in some book somewhere that I've managed to miss all my life?

B: Not at all . . .

A: A book whose existence is known only to you? Or is it a book that you wrote? That's it, isn't it? You make all these things up, don't you? You sit around thinking up restrictions and then you impose them on the people around you.

B: I do not. Everybody knows things like that.

A: I don't.

B: Then maybe you should read more.

A: Ah ha! So they are in books.

B: Some of them, but . . . listen, I don't want to talk about this anymore.

A: You brought it up.

B: I certainly did not.

A: Of course you did. You told me that we should not talk about religion and politics and then you . . .

B: I was just trying to suggest that . . .

A: You were trying to limit what we talk about.

B: No, I . . .

A: Is that it? Are you hiding a secret? Something about your religion?

B: No.

A: Or your politics? What difference would it make?

B: It wouldn't make any difference. Or shouldn't. But I'm not hiding anything. I'm trying to keep from arguing.

A: Oh, I see. And only you can do that, right?

B: What is going on?

A: I am not capable of maintaining a stable conversation. Is that what you're suggesting?

B: Well, I'm beginning to wonder.

A: How patronizing.

B: Maybe it is, but it's the truth in this case. You're saying some very illogical things, and I don't think you're doing a very mature job of . . .

A: Go on. Of what?

B: Carrying on a conversation.

A: That's not what you were going to say.

B: Yes, it was.

A: I can tell. I can always tell. You're hiding something.

B: I'm leaving.

A: Running away, are you?

B: From what?

A: From the issue.

B: What exactly is the issue?

A: You know.

B: I don't. And you've forgotten, haven't you?

A: I haven't. Yes, I have.

B: Honestly.

A: I just get so nervous.

B: About what?

A: You know.

B: Don't be. It's all going to be fine.

A: But . . .

B: What?

A: I've never been in love before.

B: But you are now?

A: Yes. Oh, yes.

B: Well, it's time . . .

——————————— • • • ———————————

Scenes for Three Actors

SCENE 11

• •

Conflict builds differently among three people than between two. Find out how the **rhythms** in this scene vary. Can you discover which character seems to be most in control? Are two in closer contact, leaving one who tends to be an outsider? How does that affect rhythm? Each of these three characters seems annoyed with the other two, and there seems to be no common purpose or **objective**. How do you go about *creating* purpose? How do you ensure that fighting does not become repetitive and go out of control? What happens when two or more people talk at the same time? How is vocal clarity maintained? Will you have to use more **vocal energy**? How do you motivate the pause when another character interrupts and you have to wait to continue what you were saying?

A: Over here . . .

B: Where?

A: Here. Right here.

B: Are you sure?

C: Do you realize how many times you've said that?

B: What?

A: Come on. Right here. I'm sure there's a . . .

C: Nothing. Never mind.

B: No, I want to hear. How many times I've said what?

C: Skip it.

A: Oh, never mind. False alarm.

B: Tell me!

C: "Are you sure?" That's what. You've said "Are you sure?" five hundred times today.

B: Well, what's wrong with that?

A: Let's look over here.

C: Nothing, I guess, if somebody says it once or twice or three times, but . . .

A: Yeah, this looks promising.

C: . . . five hundred times is a bit much.

B: Maybe you're just too demanding, you ever think of that?

C: Oh, right. It's my fault.

B: I mean, maybe you should just not try to boss people around so much.

C: Boss people around? Me? Listen, I am the world's . . .

A: Oh, yes. I think this is it. It looks like . . .

C: . . . easiest person to get along with.

B: Right.

C: Right! I can't believe you're trying to blame me for your . . .

A: . . . somebody may have been here before us, though. And if they have . . .

C: . . . lack of consideration.

A: . . . then we may have to look harder.

B: I'm easygoing too, but when somebody pushes me too hard, then I get mad.

A: But that's okay, we might still . . .

C: Oh, really? You get mad, do you?

A: . . . get what we want.

B: Yes, I do.

C: So it's okay for you to get mad, but I can't?

B: Give me a break.

C: Is that what you're saying?

A: What is the matter with you two?

B: No, it is not what I'm saying.

A: Why don't we concentrate on the job we came here to do?

C: Well, what exactly are you saying, then?

A: Instead of fighting.

B: I just think you ask too much from people.

C: Asking for a little consideration is too much?

A: I hate fights.

B: You ask more than that.

A: I just want to . . .

B: A lot more.

C: Like what?

A: . . . get on with the job.

B: Well, you want everybody to be just like you.

C: Don't be silly.

B: It's true. And the least little thing . . .

A: Peace and quiet is all I ask.

B: . . . gets on your nerves.

C: Least little thing? Repeating "Are you sure?" five hundred times is a least little thing?

B: You're exaggerating, of course.

A: Quiet.

C: Oh, I am, am I?

B: Yes, you are.

A: Quiet!

C: Well, maybe you should . . .

B: And exaggeration drives me crazy!

A: Both of you shut up!

C: What?

B: Who do you think you're shouting at?

A: You!

B: Me?

C: Yes, you.

A: Both of you!

B: Well, who do you think you are?

A: I'm sick of this squabbling.

C: Oh, yeah?

B: What squabbling?

A: If the two of you can't . . .

B: You hear that?

A: . . . behave yourselves . . .

C: I certainly did.

A: . . . I'm going to go off by myself . . .

B: The very idea.

A: . . . and let the two of you fight it out . . .

C: Some nerve.

A: . . . between yourselves.

B: Come on. Let's get out of here.

C: Right.

B: Rudest thing I ever heard.

C: Well, some people, you know . . .

Heronica

SCENE 12

• •

At first it seems that this is a fairly congenial group—at least they have a common purpose. What is this purpose? What do they see? Does personal antagonism, when it happens, come from environmental fear? Or is it built into your characterization? What effect do your choices concerning the sources of antagonism have on the build of the confrontation? Is there a leader to this group? Does that make the scene build more strongly? How do you make repetitive language have variety? Are there sometimes reasons when language should not have variety but should sound repetitive to the audience?

A: Wait a minute.

B: What?

A: What was that?

C: What?

B: What was what?

A: That noise. Listen.

C: I don't hear anything.

B: Me neither.

A: Okay. No. I guess it wasn't anything.

C: Don't do that.

A: Sorry.

C: Scare me to death.

B: Well, I guess you can't be too careful in a place like this.

C: Yeah, but don't go around spreading false alarms.

A: I said I was sorry.

B: I am not loving this.

C: It was your idea.

B: It was not.

C: It certainly was.

B: It was not. It was not!

A: Actually, it wasn't.

C: Don't you start.

A: Well, it wasn't.

B: You're nuts. I would never think up something like this.

C: Right.

A: Both of you shut up.

C: Don't tell me to shut up.

B: Shut up yourself.

A: There it is!

B: Where? Where?

C: Where? Where?

A: There. There!

C: That's not it!

B: Where?

A: It is. It is!

C: It's not, it's not!

B: Watch out!

A: I guess that wasn't it.

B: No.

C: I told you.

A: Oh, shut up.

C: Don't tell me to shut up.

B: Who do you think you are?

C: You're always telling people to shut up.

A: You're driving me crazy, both of you.

B: Same to you.

C: Look, is that a person or a . . .

A: What?

B: Where?

C: Over there.

A: That's it!

C: It is!

B: That's it, all right.

C: Now what are we going to . . .

A: Do you think we should just walk up and ask?

B: We can't.

C: We can't just walk up and ask.

A: Why not?

C: Can we?

A: Why not? You are both so . . .

B: You mean you want us to just . . .

A: . . . negative.

B: . . . walk up and ask?

A: Yes.

C: I don't know . . .

B: Honestly.

A: No, really.

B: That's incredibly naive.

C: Not to mention risky.

A: Risky?

C: Absolutely.

B: Exactly.

A: Why risky?

C: Are you kidding?

B: Sh. Wait a minute. Something's happening.

C: Besides, who'd ask?

B: Sh!

C: I'm not going to ask.

B: Sh!

A: What's happening?

B: Look.

A: Oh, yeah.

C: Wow.

B: Yeah.

A: Where's it coming from?

B: I don't know. Maybe . . .

C: Look at that!

A: I am.

B: That's big.

A: Yeah.

C: And you want us to just walk up and ask . . .

A: All right, all right . . .

B: I mean, that's big!

C: Hush, listen . . .

A: What?

C: I thought I heard . . .

B: Maybe it's an optical illusion.

A: Sure. Right.

C: Listen, I thought I heard . . .

A: Don't worry. It's not really there, we're just hallucinating.

C: . . . some kind of noise.

B: All right, all right.

C: There! Listen!

B: Oh, my God!

C: Watch out!

A: Run!

C: Get out of the way!

A: Run! Run!

B: This way! Don't go that way, that's the wrong way, idiot!

C: Wait!

A: What!

C: It's gone.

B: Well . . .

A: What do you know . . .

C: Can you beat that?

A: Come on.

B: Amazing.

A: Let's try over there.

B: Okay.

C: Incredible.

A: Maybe we'll find it again. Or another one.

C: Yeah.

B: I hate this.

C: It was your idea.

B: It was not!

A: Oh, shut up.

SCENE 13

• •

Here's a group with what seems to be a long-standing history. In what ways is their confrontation based on that background? There is a natural leader, it seems, on whom the build centers. Does this person's charisma and authority precipitate the conflict? Then, of course, there is the project they've embarked on: What is it? Why is it so difficult? Will it be accomplished? In what ways will physical activity affect the confrontation's build? Watch out for apparently abrupt transitions; be sure they are well grounded in subtextual motivation.

A: Okay, let's try it one more time.

B: Do we have to?

A: We do if we're ever going to get it right.

B: I'm not sure if I'm up to this.

C: Me neither.

A: Of course you are. Now come on, put a little energy into it this time.

C: It'll never happen.

A: Well . . .

C: See? I told you.

B: I give up.

C: Me, too.

A: No, no. We can't give up.

C: Oh, yes we can.

B: I just did.

A: All right, fine. Just walk away. I don't care. What's it to me? If you guys want to be the kind of people who give in at the least little obstacle, then I guess that's the way it's going to have to be. There are plenty of others who are very happy to take your place.

B: Oh, yeah? Like who?

A: Plenty of others.

C: Name two. Name one.

B: You can't, because there aren't any others.

A: Yes, there are, too.

C: Oh, please . . .

B: It's just impossible.

C: It can't be done.

B: Everybody sees that but you.

C: Everybody.

A: Do you remember when we were little kids, and we decided to run away from home? All three of us? You remember that?

B: . . . yeah.

C: Sure. So what?

A: Well, we got as far as the city limits and there weren't any houses anymore and you two got scared.

C: No way.

B: I didn't.

A: And both of you wanted to go back home. And I said, no, we've got to go on, once we've started something, we've got to finish it. But all you two could do was cry.

C: I didn't cry.

B: We weren't crying.

A: Of course you were. Both of you. Anyway, I pulled out some peanut butter and mayonnaise sandwiches and we stopped and ate them and then we went on.

B: Oh, yeah.

C: Right.

A: Remember?

C: I remember the peanut butter and mayonnaise sandwiches.

A: So. That's what we have to do now.

B: You're going to whip out a batch of peanut butter and . . .

A: No, no, no. I'm saying we've got to stop and rest and . . .

C: The only difference is this: it was a mistake to run away from home then and this is . . .

A: What do you want?

C: Just what I said. It was a . . .

A: We did it, didn't we?

B: No, we did not. We walked another quarter of a mile and then we went back home, that's what we . . .

C: Right. If we'd really run away from home we wouldn't be . . .

A: You just don't get the point, do you?

B: You're the one that doesn't get the point. Ever since we were little you've been . . .

C: How could we have run away from home?

B: . . . leading us around by the nose, getting us to do things we didn't want to do.

C: Like eat peanut butter and . . .

B: Right.

C: . . . mayonnaise sandwiches.

B: Which we both hated, but you . . .

C: Despised! But you were . . .

B: . . . liked. So because you liked them . . .

C: . . . crazy about them!

B: . . . we had to eat them.

A: You don't have to do anything you don't want to do.

B: How many times have we heard that before?

C: Zillions.

B: Come on, let's go swim the Bosporus.

A: All right, all right, all right . . .

C: Paint the pyramids blue.

B: Hang-glide off the Golden Gate Bridge.

C: Become a movie star.

B: Get rich overnight.

A: I don't want to hear anymore!

C: That's the way it's always been.

B: You're not happy unless you're bossing somebody around.

A: Shut up!

B: Well, we've had it.

C: No more.

A: Fine. Get out. Go away.

B: Wait a minute, what's that?

C: Is that . . . ?

A: Yes. And after lunch . . .

B: Oh, no.

A: . . . we'll try it again. Right?

C: Yeah, yeah . . .

A: And this time we'll get it right!

B: Oh God, I hate this.

C: Me, too.

SCENE 14

• •

Here is a situation that gives free rein to the imagination. Two of the characters seem to be in league against the third. Don't make assumptions that lead in only one direction, however. Base choices on careful examination of the text and exploration of the subtext, and let the confrontation develop from there. And in determining environment, remember that the most obvious choice isn't necessarily always the best. How excited does character C become? Do characters A and B join in that excitement? For the same reasons? Don't rush transitions, find the pauses and the thoughts that fill them.

A: Get in.

B: Now.

C: Huh? What?

B: Do what you're told. Get in.

A: Now.

C: But . . .

A: Does this convince you that we're not playing around?

C: . . . yes.

A: I thought it would.

B: Now then, isn't this better?

A: Cozier?

B: More comfortable?

A: You're not cold, are you?

B: Or too warm, maybe?

C: Who are you?

A: Friends.

B: Absolutely.

A: Don't worry.

B: About anything.

C: I'm not worried, I just . . .

A: You are, though.

B: We can tell.

C: Okay, I'm worried. A little.

A: Confess. You're worried a lot.

C: Uh . . . maybe.

A: Of course.

B: Now we're getting somewhere.

C: Where?

B: Hm?

C: Where, exactly, are we getting to?

A: Don't worry about that now.

C: But . . .

A: I mean, it's beyond your control, isn't it?

C: Well, apparently . . .

B: Of course it is.

A: But you're right, in a way. We do have to establish some goals, don't we?

B: Oh, yes.

A: Some procedures.

B: Absolutely.

C: I guess.

A: So we might as well begin.

B: Good.

A: Now. Do you remember the night of your eighteenth birthday party?

C: My eighteenth . . .

A: You were at the lake and you had a little too much to drink. So you left the others and walked out on to that grassy patch by the boathouse and sat on the bench there. The red one.

C: How did you know about . . .

B: Just relax now.

A: You lit a cigarette—you were still smoking then—and were just getting your head to work properly, when you saw the lights.

B: They didn't frighten you exactly, but they did disturb you.

A: Not at first, of course.

B: No, at first you thought they were . . .

C: Airplanes.

B: Yes. But then they stopped moving, right?

C: Yes. They stopped. Dead still.

B: For about . . .

A: Half an hour? Would you say?

C: It seemed like that long. But it couldn't have been, could it?

B: And then they all started moving closer to each other until there was one large light, isn't that correct?

C: A very large light. A very large blue light.

B: Which began to get bigger, didn't it? Bigger and bigger?

C: Yes. Very big. It got very big indeed.

A: And then it landed on the lake?

B: And you were frightened.

C: I was. I was scared.

A: But you went in anyway, didn't you?

B: When the door opened?

A: When they asked you to come in?

C: Yes. I went in. When they asked me to.

B: Now here's what we want to know. What did the inside look like? Was it a large room? Was there a great deal of light? Or was it dark? Were there people standing around in it or was it empty? What can you tell us?

A: Describe the room. In as much detail as you can. Starting . . .

B: Now.

C: The room was circular in shape and was quite large. If you imagine a round basketball court, you'll have some idea how big it was. And it had a shiny floor like a basketball court, and, yes, there were marks on the floor like painted lines and . . . but it wasn't.

A: Wasn't a basketball court.

C: No.

B: No. We didn't think so.

C: And there were . . . people in it.

B: Many of them?

C: Yes. Twenty or so. But not all alike.

A: Ah.

C: Oh, no. Very different.

B: Their skin?

C: Most of them had tan skins . . . golden, maybe, would be a better way to describe it. And they had peculiar eyes, I thought.

A: But you could have been imagining that.

C: Maybe. Some of them looked rather like you.

A: I'm sure you're imagining that.

C: Maybe . . . but . . .

A: I mean, who do you think you are?

B: Yes. Do you think of us as a threat?

A: A danger to you? In some way?

C: I'm starting to. I'm starting to get really . . .

A: Scared?

C: Yes!

B: Calm down now.

C: I don't feel like calming down.

A: But you must.

B: Absolutely.

C: No! I want to get out of here!

A: What did the people in the room do to you?

B: Did they threaten you in some way?

C: They poked me!

A: Poked you? With what?

C: Sticks! Like that one!

A: You're imagining things.

C: No, no! I'm not! That stick! That one!

B: There's no stick.

C: And it shocked me! It hurt me! Like that!

B: You're safe.

A: Perfectly safe. Nobody's hurting you.

C: . . . am I?

A: Don't be afraid.

B: Everything's all right.

C: Is it?

A: Of course.

B: Just relax.

C: . . . yes.

B: Take care now.

A: We'll see you again . . .

• • • •

CHARACTER CONSTRUCTION

Characterization is the actor's basic task. The person in the play lives a life as individual as the actor's own, yet only an hour or two of words must provide a basis for the construction and assimilation of this new life. Perhaps the first job is for you to know yourselves well: How do you *really* look? How much do you *really* weigh? How tall (or short) are you, *really*? When you know the *real* answers to these questions, you can begin to know the physical raw material you have to invest in the character's incarnation. Then begins the very complicated task of dredging up biography and motivation and emotion from the words the playwright has given you. You must do a thorough job of understanding the subtext and writing your **character analysis**. Do some outside research if necessary. Write a complete birth-to-death **character biography**. Find the way the character moves and speaks and work on ways your own body can physicalize this. Then allow yourself to be possessed.

------------------------------ • • • ------------------------------

Scenes for Two Actors

SCENE 15

• •

How much can be learned about characters from the way they speak? Do they express themselves formally or casually? Do they use slang or are their words carefully chosen, framed in correct and precise grammar? Does their mode of speech, perhaps, merely reflect the immediate situation in which they find themselves and not, perhaps, their customary way of speaking? How do you decide that? How old are these characters? Is their apparent age consistent with what seems to be their approach to life? How long have the characters known each other? What brings them together on this occasion? What is their educational level? Their economic situation? Are they on better terms with each other at the end of the scene than at the beginning? Worse?

A: Would you please hand me that bowl?

B: Of course.

A: Thank you so much.

B: Anything else I can do?

A: Certainly not. You just make yourself comfortable.

B: Are you sure? Look, I could . . .

A: No, please don't. It isn't necessary.

B: Honestly now . . .

A: I find it so much easier to do it myself.

B: Oh. Of course.

A: If you don't mind.

B: No, no. Not at all. I was just . . .

A: Of course.

B: It certainly has been a pleasant day. As soon as I got out of work I started to get my train, and all of a sudden—pure impulse really—I decided to go to the park. Silly of me, I suppose. But once I'd gotten there and found an empty bench, it was as if I couldn't move. The sun just paralyzed me, and I actually found myself relaxing. I think I even shut my eyes for a moment . . .

A: How nice.

B: Well, you know, it was. Not the kind of thing I'd be tempted to do often. Haven't for years. But for once, well . . .

A: Perhaps you should.

B: Pardon?

A: Perhaps you should do it more often.

B: Do you think so?

A: Am I being presumptuous?

B: No, no. Not at all.

A: I thought you looked rather . . . strained. That's all.

B: I have been rather busy.

A: Of course.

B: Still, there's no reason for me not to indulge myself once in a while. Take a moment or two off. Watch the world go by, as it were. That's what you meant?

A: Well, yes. Of course, I may go too far in the other direction. Perhaps I'm not ambitious enough.

B: Oh, I'm sure . . .

A: No, no. I'm perfectly ready to admit it. I'm simply not strongly motivated toward worldly success. I drift. I've never held a job for longer than eighteen months in my life.

B: Really?

A: Don't be alarmed. I've never been fired, either. I just get bored easily. Fortunately, I've never had to worry about money.

B: No.

A: Still, here I am at this point in my life, and I look around and wonder what it all adds up to.

B: You lead a very comfortable life, I'm sure, and . . .

A: You have children, don't you?

B: Oh, yes.

A: How wonderful that must be.

B: I suppose so. But you know, I don't see them very often. As a matter of fact, I might go so far as to say that we don't get along very well.

A: How is that possible?

B: Very possible, I'm afraid. But you see, it doesn't automatically follow that simply because people are genetically related, they are going to be congenial. In fact, sometimes I feel it works to the contrary. Of course, it makes for loneliness . . .

A: Come now, how can you have been lonely?

B: I assure you that I have.

A: I thought I was the only one.

B: Maybe everybody assumes everybody else's life to be less lonely than their own.

A: Perhaps. That's a comforting thought.

B: Is it?

A: Yes. You've made me feel better.

B: Better than you expected?

A: I had no expectations.

B: No, I guess I didn't either. Now that you mention it.

A: So . . .

B: You sure I can't help?

A: Absolutely not. All done, in fact. See?

B: Yes! Wonderful . . .

A: You think so?

B: I certainly do.

A: So do I . . .

Scene 16
••

It should be easy to determine the age of the two characters in this scene. But don't be surprised if age can be more variable than it seems at first glance. *What* these people are doing may be the determining factor in deciding their ages; once the activity is decided, their ages may follow. An interesting aspect of this scene is that the characters speak from a relatively simple subtext. Almost everything they say can be said in a manner that is devoid of deception—guileless. Given that, it is a useful exercise in **present-tense acting**, allowing you to concentrate on **reality level**, that is, making the characters true to life. If subtext were created to make these characters more complex—and that is certainly possible—then the scene would become more of an exercise in the invention of characterizational subtext. If you create such subtext, make sure your subtextual choices are appropriate and firmly grounded in the text.

A: That's mine.

B: It is not.

A: It is.

B: Well, can I use it?

A: No.

B: Why not?

A: Because it's mine.

B: But you're not using it.

A: Yes, I am.

B: No, you're not.

A: I am now.

B: You're weird.

A: Look who's talking.

B: I'm talking, that's who.

A: 'Cause you're scared.

B: I am not.

A: Yes, you are.

B: You're not, right?

A: Yeah . . . a little.

B: What do you think's going to happen?

A: Well . . .

B: Are we going to have fun?

A: Sure.

B: How do you know? You've never done this before.

A: Sure I have.

B: When?

A: Before.

B: Where? Here?

A: Uh-uh. Somewhere else.

B: I don't believe you. Liar, liar . . .

A: Liar yourself. I did it.

B: What was it like, then? Tell me.

A: No.

B: Then you didn't do it.

A: Oh, all right. At first I was really scared . . .

B: I knew it.

A: But then, after I got used to it, I wasn't scared anymore. Then it was fun. Of course, you have to hold on really tight.

B: Really?

A: Sure. It goes on and on. Then it gets faster and faster.

B: I didn't know it got faster.

A: Then it slows down. Then, all of a sudden, it's over.

B: Then what do you do?

A: Whatever you were doing before. Course, you have to clean up.

B: Clean up?

A: Yeah. Sometimes.

B: I didn't know there'd be anything to clean up.

A: Sure. Sometimes.

B: I don't think I want to do this. I think I'm going to go on home now.

A: You can't just . . .

B: Yeah, I can. I never wanted to do this in the first place. You were the one that talked me into it, but I didn't know you'd done it before.

A: What difference does that make?

B: Well, if I'm the only one who's never done it before, then I'll probably be the only one to do it wrong and mess it up and get laughed at.

A: Nobody's going to laugh at you.

B: Yes, they will. If I do something stupid, I want to do it with somebody else who'll do something stupid, too.

A: Okay, I promise I'll do something stupid, then.

B: You will?

A: Yeah.

B: Promise?

A: Promise.

B: Well . . .

A: Come on. You'll love it. Besides, you might as well go on and get the first time over with now that you've come this far.

B: I guess.

A: Sure.

B: Can I use that?

A: It's mine.

B: I know. But you're done using it. So can I use it?

SCENE 17

• •

This scene is particularly rich in subtextual possibilities. The most interesting approach is to build a rational subtextual framework that explains and justifies the apparent contradictions and nonsequiturs in the text. Don't immediately come to the conclusion that either of the characters is mentally unbalanced, as irrational dialogue doesn't always derive from mental disturbance. It is the actor's job to make the progression of the character's thoughts clear to the audience, whatever mental set such thoughts come from. This is also a good scene to work on environment construction. Don't be tempted to have the characters simply sitting and talking. Motivated movement is more of a challenge and will be valuable in communicating meaning to the audience.

A: I always felt that I could rely on him. But he let me down.

B: Are you sure?

A: Oh, yes. He let me down all right. Badly.

B: How?

A: Well, for instance, he said he would recommend me for promotion, then I found out later that he didn't.

B: How did you find out?

A: I have my sources.

B: So you didn't get promoted?

A: No. In fact, I got laid off.

B: You were fired?

A: Laid off.

B: Isn't that the same as getting fired?

A: I guess, yeah.

B: And you blame him?

A: He said he'd recommend me, and he didn't.

B: And that was the reason you got fired instead of promoted?

A: Yes.

B: What would you say if I told you that he did, in fact, recommend you for promotion?

A: I wouldn't believe you.

B: Here's a copy of the letter.

A: This is a forgery.

B: Why do you say that?

A: Because he did not recommend me.

B: But he did. Here is the letter.

A: It's a forgery, I tell you. Why do you make up lies like this?

B: The letter is not a forgery.

A: Everybody always lies to me. Why is that?

B: You think everybody lies to you?

A: I know it. I know they do. Why do they? Can you tell me that?

B: I'm afraid I can't.

A: Why not?

B: Because I don't believe it's true.

A: You think I'm lying?

B: I think you're mistaken.

A: I thought you were on my side.

B: I am.

A: You're not if you accuse me of lying.

B: I didn't say you were lying. I said you were . . .

A: Oh, I know how it goes. You're probably the one who told my boss that I stole some paper clips.

B: No, I didn't. I didn't even know you had stolen some paper clips.

A: I didn't. But somebody said I did. That's why I got laid off.

B: I thought you got laid off because there was no letter of recommendation from . . .

A: It was a combination of factors.

B: I see.

A: So, how've you been?

B: Fine, thank you.

A: No more problems with the government?

B: No.

A: You're lying.

B: Why would I want to do that?

A: Maybe you're a spy.

B: Don't be silly.

A: A foreign agent. In times of war there are always spies around.

B: Granted. But why do you think I'm one?

A: You have forged documents.

B: This letter?

A: Yes.

B: It isn't forged.

A: It is. Do you know how I know?

B: No. Tell me.

A: You misspelled his name.

B: A typographical error.

A: Three times? Look here. And here, and here . . .

B: Yes, but . . .

A: A pretty stupid mistake, considering that you've known both of us for so long.

B: All right, you've got me. Where does that leave us?

A: Back where we started. Someone's been putting something in my food to make me paranoid.

B: You think so, do you?

A: Yes. Which proves that I'm paranoid, doesn't it?

B: I would think so. Unless your food really is poison.

A: What should I do?

B: Don't think about it right now. Eat your dinner.

A: I can't. It's radioactive.

B: How did you find out about that?

SCENE 18

• •

Before deciding on a specific point of view for this scene, experiment with a variety of characterizational choices. Don't automatically assume that one character is sympathetic and the other not. Remember that good characterization depends on a mixture of motivations—some positive, some negative. In constructing your biographies of these characters, find the good and bad in each. Does one of them perhaps have an accent? In what way might regional or even national differences enter into the playing of the character? Is English not the usual language of character B? Try using contractions instead of the more formal constructions that character B uses. What effect does this lessening of formality in speech have on the character and therefore on the scene? Is this a temporary relationship or one that has been established for a while? Try experimenting with the ages of the characters and see how that affects subtext.

A: Could you sit down for a moment?

B: I am restless.

A: I can see that, but I've got something to tell you.

B: What is that?

A: Sit down.

B: I am not in the mood.

A: You don't even know what I'm going to say. How do you know you're not in the mood to hear it?

B: I just know, that is all. My mind is . . .

A: We've got to talk.

B: I am . . .

A: Upset?

B: No. It is more like . . .

A: Do you have a fever?

B: How would I know?

A: You look like you've been hyperventilating.

B: Well, appearances can be deceiving.

A: Look, I'm leaving.

B: Why are you going to do that?

A: For very complicated reasons.

B: Even so, I would like to know them.

A: Well, part of it is that you and I don't get along very well.

B: What do you mean?

A: We're very different people, you and I. We don't . . . speak the same language.

B: How can you say that?

A: There're just too many differences.

B: Like what?

A: Oh, just . . . it's too difficult to explain.

B: I think you have to try.

A: That's one of them.

B: What is? What are you talking about?

A: You keep pushing me.

B: Pushing you? What exactly do you mean by that?

A: You're too . . . persistent.

B: Explain.

A: No. I don't want to explain any further.

B: That is not logical.

A: Maybe not, but it's the way I feel.

B: So you are leaving without an explanation?

A: Yes. I am.

B: Not only illogical. It is rude.

A: Sorry.

B: Nobody ever called me pushy before.

A: I didn't say pushy, exactly.

B: But that is what you meant.

A: I guess so.

B: Which just goes to show that Americans are not very perceptive.

A: Oh?

B: Just because I tried to raise your consciousness a little, you accuse me of being too aggressive.

A: See, I don't think I need my consciousness raised.

B: Of course not. How could you know? You are not sensitive enough.

A: That doesn't sound the least bit egotistical to you?

B: No, it is just honest.

A: Look, I can understand how you would have hurt feelings, but you must . . .

B: My feelings are not hurt.

A: But I don't mean it to be insulting or anything.

B: I am not insulted. I am merely curious at your illogical behavior.

A: I just want to change my environment.

B: Very well. I am not stopping you.

A: Okay. Fine. Then I'm going.

B: But what have I done wrong?

SCENE 19

• •

In this scene, the first thing you should do is determine not only the characters' ages but their physical and mental capacities as well. This is an opportunity to use a considerable amount of imagination in developing these aspects of characterization. Are the characters related? Are they planning a real theft or is it imaginary? What are their limitations and how do they affect characterization? How nervous are they? If this is a real event, how do you explain the erratic and varying levels of their expertise and intelligence?

A: If we go in this way, won't they see us?

B: I don't think so.

A: Why not?

B: Well, it'll be dark, for one thing.

A: But there are lights there.

B: We can take the bulbs out.

A: How?

B: Go in the day before and just take them out.

A: Won't they notice?

B: I don't think so.

A: I'm scared.

B: Me, too.

A: Then why are we doing this?

B: We don't have any choice. If we don't do it, we'll never amount to anything.

A: What's wrong with that?

B: And besides, we've got to get the picture.

A: Yeah. Right. I know.

B: So, we'll go in this way.

A: Okay. Then what?

B: Up the stairs.

A: How many flights?

B: Twelve.

A: Twelve?

B: I know it's a lot, but we can't risk the elevators.

A: I know, I know.

B: You'll just have to get in better shape.

A: All right, all right.

B: Once we get into the apartment, we'll be all right.

A: Will we?

B: Sure. But first we have to disable the alarm system.

A: How do we do that?

B: Are you kidding? That was supposed to be your job.

A: Oh. Right.

B: So, do you know?

A: What?

B: How to disable the alarm system!

A: Oh. Yeah. Sure.

B: So?

A: Just leave it to me. I'll attach my portable computer to it and figure out the code. Don't worry about it.

B: How long will it take?

A: Less than ninety seconds.

B: You sure?

A: Sure. Don't worry about it. I'm all checked out.

B: I worry. But anyway, we get inside, then we have to get the picture.

A: What if somebody's at home?

B: We've talked about this over and over again. When are you going to get it straight? We stand outside and watch them get in the limo. We don't go in until we see that.

A: Oh, yeah. I forgot.

B: Now, once we get the picture, you've got to be sure it isn't a forgery.

A: I'm going to do that?

B: Of course. I can't do it. You're the only one that can.

A: Right.

B: You got all your equipment to do that with?

A: Do I?

B: Well, why don't you check your bag?

A: Oh, yeah. Yeah. I got it.

B: How long will it take you to verify the picture?

A: Couple minutes.

B: Then all we have to do is leave.

A: Yeah. I'll be glad of that.

B: We both will.

A: You feeling okay?

B: Not really.

A: You want your medicine?

B: Thanks.

A: I wish Mom would come home.

B: Why?

A: So she can fix us some soup.

B: You fix it.

A: She won't let me use the can opener.

B: I'll do it.

A: You can't reach it.

SCENE 20

• •

It would seem that these two people are very different. Find in the words they use and the way they use them the differences in their social and educational standing. The identity of the object the characters speak of is less important than the sense of curiosity on one side and pride of ownership on the other. There is also, as the text indicates, an age disparity; but is it as much as one character alleges? Environment is important, too. Where are they, and how does that affect the nature of their conversation? Are there witnesses? How exactly do you create the feeling of a specific environment through voice and body alone?

A: Could I speak to you for a moment?

B: What's your problem?

A: Does this belong to you?

B: What?

A: This.

B: Oh. Yeah. Gimme it.

A: What is it?

B: Huh?

A: What exactly is it?

B: What does it look like?

A: It would appear to have some vague relationship to a finial.

B: Huh?

A: It looks like a finial.

B: What's a finial?

A: The object at the top of a lamp that holds the shade on.

B: Never heard of it.

A: That's not what it is?

B: Nope.

A: Then . . .

B: What do you want to know for?

A: Curiosity.

B: Yeah, well, maybe you should mind your own business.

A: I assure you I didn't mean to pry.

B: Oh, yeah.

A: Honestly. It's only that I have always had a natural affinity for investigation. Things intrigue me, and I like to follow a logical path to ascertaining their function. Don't you find such preoccupations rewarding?

B: What I find rewarding is a few extra bucks, and that's exactly what I was heading for when you butted in with all this bunch of questions.

A: There really is no need to be rude.

B: You ain't heard rude. Where I come from you know rude right away when you hear it.

A: Where do you come from?

B: There you go again.

A: Pardon?

B: Sticking your nose in where it don't belong. What does it matter to you where I come from? It ever occur to you that it ain't a swell idea to go around filling a total stranger in on everything about your whole life?

A: I merely asked . . .

B: You spend a little time on the streets, and you'll find out quick enough that the less other people know about you, the safer you are. You can't just go around trusting everybody you know.

A: I think maybe you can.

B: Oh, you do, huh?

A: Well, I think maybe trust is something that has to be offered as a kind of guarantee that you mean no harm.

B: I gotta tell you then, I'm real surprised you've lasted as long as you obviously have.

A: You think of me as old?

B: Sure. You got to be pushing . . .

A: Perception varies. Perhaps you need to expand your horizons.

B: Yeah, like you need to expand the distance between us, maybe.

A: You want me to leave?

B: That's the idea.

A: You realize I have as much right to be here as you do.

B: Feeling pretty cocky, huh?

A: Well, I'm not afraid, if that's what you . . .

B: Maybe you should be.

A: I don't think so.

B: Think again. You don't even recognize something dangerous when you see it.

A: Like what?

B: Like this . . . what'd you call it? A fin gill?

A: Finial.

B: Whatever. Anyway, it ain't got nothing to do with lampshades. This is what it does.

A: Oh, my God . . .

SCENE 21

• •

This scene is based on a major transition for one of the characters. Find the argument in the basic situation that allows for a change of mind, then permit characterization to be formed from that. It is also important that you don't allow the scene to become clichéd or maudlin. Find the solution to difficult transitions that are, perhaps, not so obvious as might first occur to you. Experiment with variations on what is apparently a physical limitation in one of the characters. Is it real? Exaggerated? How do you physicalize it? Must you do some research to find out? Don't jump to conclusions. Be creative and imaginative.

A: Can you reach it?

B: No.

A: Do you want me to . . .

B: No.

A: It's no trouble.

B: If I want help, I'll ask for it.

A: All right.

B: Would you give it to me?

A: Yes. Of course.

B: Not that way.

A: Sorry.

B: Watch out!

A: Sorry.

B: Never mind, never mind.

A: I'll clean it up.

B: Forget it.

A: I don't mind.

B: Right. You probably don't.

A: I don't. Honestly.

B: And you think I'm going to be grateful, don't you?

A: I wasn't thinking about that. I certainly wasn't expecting you to be
. . .

B: Well, I'm not.

A: Fine.

B: You have any idea how many people are standing around just
dying to look like a good samaritan? Whether you know it or not,
there are a lot of people who need to feel superior to somebody
else, and they go out of their way to find pathetic cases to stand
next to for five minutes so they can look good.

A: Is that what you consider yourself? A pathetic case?

B: Oh, you don't understand. None of you ever understands.

A: I'm trying to.

B: No, you're not. You're trying to look good.

A: No, I'm not. And if you could be reasonable for a second or two
and let me explain . . .

B: I'm being unreasonable, am I?

A: Well, I don't think you're giving me a fair chance, anyway.

B: Why don't you just go away?

A: Is that what you want me to do?

B: What does it matter what I want?

A: It matters to me.

B: Really? Don't lie to me.

A: I'm not. I swear. Shall I go or stay?

B: Oh . . . stay.

A: Then I will. I'd also like to help you if you'd let me. No, don't interrupt. Let me finish. I'm not offering to help because I feel sorry
for you. I don't think there's any reason to feel sorry for you.
There are simply some things that I do better than you do at the
moment. And there are some things you do better than I do at the
moment. So I may be asking you to help me.

B: What do I do better than you?

A: Lots of things, I'll bet. For instance, you're very good at getting
your point of view across.

B: Okay, I'm bossy. What good is that?

A: Well, I don't think I'm very assertive, so I could learn to be more
outgoing or aggressive from you.

B: Maybe you could.

A: So, see? You help me as much as I help you.

B: Maybe.

A: You don't sound convinced.

B: See, it's very difficult for me to trust people. I suppose that's because ever since . . . for a long time now I've figured that nobody
wanted to be with me except to either feel sorry for me or patronize me. I can't handle either.

A: No reason why you should.

B: So . . . you're saying we could be . . . friends?

A: Of course.

B: Well . . . could you help me with this, please?

A: Delighted.

B: . . . thanks.

Scene 22

• •

Here are two characters whose concerns are immediate issues: where they will stay, what they will eat. Are they homeless "street people" or are they simply on vacation? Perhaps the first thing to do with this scene is to test the limits of choice. How many different ways can the scene be played? These choices can be about environment and financial status, but they can also be about such character traits as stubbornness, leadership, sense of humor, and the status of an apparently troubled relationship. Try switching the strength level from character to character. How does the scene differ when dominance is reversed?

A: What about tonight?

B: What about it?

A: Where are we going to stay?

B: I don't know.

A: When will you know?

B: Why do I have to be the one to decide?

A: You always do.

B: Do I?

A: You know you do.

B: Well, then, I'll think about it.

A: Think about food, too.

B: What about it?

A: Stop saying that.

B: Stop saying what?

A: "What about it."

B: What?

A: "What about it." Stop saying "What about it."

B: Oh. Do I say that a lot?

A: Yes.

B: I didn't realize that.

A: So what about food?

B: What ab . . . I mean . . .

A: You were going to say it again, weren't you?

B: No, I swear I wasn't.

A: So are we going to eat?

B: Are you ready?

A: Yes. I'm hungry. Aren't you?

B: I guess.

A: So . . .

B: I don't know why I have to make all these decisions. I hate to make decisions.

A: You do not.

B: Oh, yes. I do.

A: You want me to decide, then?

B: Yes. You decide.

A: Okay, we'll buy some stuff at a grocery and go back to the . . .

B: You mean like canned stuff?

A: Well, I suppose . . .

B: I don't like canned stuff.

A: Fine, we'll get . . .

B: It always tastes like tin.

A: Then we'll get . . . a roasted chicken. How about that?

B: I don't eat chicken.

A: What do you mean, you don't eat chicken?

B: I'm a vegetarian.

A: Great. So what do you want, then?

B: Vegetables.

A: I gathered that. What kind of vegetables?

B: I don't know . . . eggplant.

A: Uh-huh. You plan to eat raw eggplant?

B: Sure. Why not?

A: Not me.

B: Raw vegetables are good for you.

A: Not raw eggplant. Not me.

B: We'll cook them, then.

A: Where?

B: I don't know. We can . . .

A: Let's go to the Burger Palace.

B: You've got to be kidding.

A: What do you mean?

B: First of all, that junk is loaded with preservatives, secondly it's loaded with fat and calories, thirdly it's loaded with germs, fourthly . . .

A: Okay, okay, I don't want to hear it.

B: But that's the problem. You stick your head in the sand about issues like nutrition and then when trouble crops up you wonder why.

A: Let me tell you something. I grew up eating fried chicken and vegetables that had been cooked for twelve hours with pieces of fatback floating around in them, and I'm healthy.

B: Maybe you are, maybe you aren't. Get your cholesterol level checked and then we'll talk.

A: Anyway, we can't exactly be too picky.

B: Why not?

A: Well, you apparently haven't noticed that we are not exactly loaded with money.

B: Oh, don't worry about money.

A: Fine. I'll pay the man at the Burger Palace with my Platinum American Express Card.

B: I didn't know you had a Platinum American . . .

A: Forget it.

B: I didn't know you had any kind of American Express . . .

A: You know something? Your attitude is really irritating me.

B: My attitude?

A: Yes!

B: What about it?

SCENE 23

• •

Transitions are the main problem in this scene. Is it possible to make both characters appear perfectly rational? Or is it necessary to base one of them, at least, in mental aberration? Frequently, actors are called on to motivate apparently illogical choices in characterizational dialogue. Remember, delusional characters believe they are being completely logical and rational. Some clichés and difficult **phrasings** are also built into the scene. Commit to them and understand that the character does not find them stereotyped. Don't patronize the characters or the way they speak. Spend some time deciding on an environment location.

A: Let's go inside.

B: Oh, no.

A: Why not?

B: I couldn't.

A: But that's what we're here for.

B: Well, just to look . . .

A: That's what I want to do: go inside and look.

B: I didn't realize we'd be actually going inside.

A: How could we look if we didn't go inside?

B: I hadn't thought . . .

A: What would we see outside?

B: Well . . . the outside.

A: That's crazy.

B: Are you calling me crazy?

A: You have to admit it's kind of weird to just look at the outside.

B: I'm not crazy.

A: Fine.

B: Just because I've spent a little time in therapy groups is no reason to brand me with that reprehensible name.

A: You know, you're really blowing this out of proportion.

B: Oh, am I? So now you're saying that I'm being irrational?

A: No, I'm . . .

B: Paranoid?

A: If you'll calm down for a moment . . .

B: Now I'm hysterical. I see. You know, people like you don't realize how much damage you do to other people. You go around walking all over people's feelings, and you don't even care. Well, let me tell you something, I'm not just going to lie down and let you trample on me. No, indeed! I'm going to fight back. You must come to your senses and be a force for good in the world, not evil! After all, someone with your obvious gifts should be constructive in your pursuits, not destructive.

A: What in the world are you talking about?

B: Pardon?

A: I said, what are you talking about? You realize you're causing a scene?

B: Me?

A: Yes, of course.

B: All I said was that I was shy about going inside.

A: I think you should go and lie down.

B: Why? I'm not tired.

A: You're not well.

B: I am. I'm perfectly fit.

A: You realize, of course, that sometimes we're not the best judge of our own condition?

B: Let's walk down this street here. Look, isn't that the famous bridge down there?

A: Sometimes it takes an outsider to tell us when something's wrong.

B: An outsider? Look at that.

A: A friend, say, or an acquaintance, even.

B: Watch out for that frog.

A: I remember once when I was very young I was being very destructive to my dog without even knowing it. See, I loved him very much, and I was letting him get away with all kinds of inappropriate behavior. In other words, he was spoiled. Well, my mother sat me down and talked to me about it and let me know that it was in the best interests of the dog to be more disciplined in his training. So I got a lot tougher with him and he was a happier dog. But it took my mother to bring that to my attention.

B: I never had a cat.

A: Neither did I.

B: Are you trying to confuse me?

A: No.

B: Yes, you are. You go on and on about your cat and then when I try to communicate, to let you know I never had that experience, you deny ever mentioning it.

A: I was talking about my dog.

B: See? There you go again.

A: I was. I was telling you about my dog.

B: I could probably go inside this one. Those look like friendly people going inside right now. Do you think they are?

A: What? Oh, yes . . . look, I really think it would be better if we went back to . . .

B: I don't think they would hurt us. And I caught a glimpse of something blue when the door opened. I'd like to see what that was. Aren't you coming?

A: I don't think that would be a good idea.

B: Come on, don't be mean.

A: Look into my eyes.

B: Huh?

A: Look into my eyes. That's right. Now, I'm going to count to ten and with each number you're going to be more and more relaxed.

B: Please don't say things like that. You're frightening me.

A: One, two, three, four . . .

B: No. I'm leaving.

A: Five, six, seven, eight . . .

B: No!

A: Nine, ten. Now. How do you feel?

B: Who are you?

SCENE 24

• •

In a shared scene of this kind it is important to make the relationship—whatever it is—believable without putting the burden of negativity on one character. As with many emotional states, it is sometimes more effective to play against the obvious. Find selfishness, for instance, in both characters. Find fear in both. Experiment with different relationships and environments.

A: I'll be back in a minute.

B: Where are you going?

A: Just down there for a moment.

B: Don't leave me alone.

A: I'll just be gone for a moment.

B: You can't leave me alone here.

A: Nobody will bother you.

B: How do you know?

A: Look, if you just sit here and mind your own business, you'll be fine.

B: No, I won't. I'll be dead by the time you come back.

A: Don't be absurd.

B: What about that guy over there?

A: He's selling apples.

B: Yes, but is that all he's doing?

A: You want to come with me?

B: No, I'm tired.

A: You just want to hang around here?

B: Why not? We don't have much longer to wait.

A: All right, all right . . .

B: Now you're mad.

A: No, no.

B: Yes, you are. You're mad.

A: It's just that I seem to spend an awful lot of time being a kind of babysitter.

B: To me, you mean?

A: Well . . .

B: I certainly don't want to be a burden.

A: It's just that I don't seem to get very much time when I can just be by myself and do what I want to do without feeling that I've abandoned you.

B: I hadn't realized I was so dependent.

A: Oh, I'm probably blowing the whole thing out of proportion. It probably doesn't happen nearly as often as I think it does.

B: Even a few times is too many.

A: Don't feel bad, now . . .

B: See, I had a really tough childhood.

A: You don't have to explain. We don't have much time . . .

B: My father abandoned my mom and me when I was just seven years old, see, and she never let me forget it. She always made me feel that I was absolutely essential to her happiness and that if I let her down, she wouldn't be able to survive.

A: I guess a lot of mothers put people through that kind of guilt process.

B: When I went off to college, she killed herself.

A: No!

B: Absolutely. It made quite an impact on me. From that time on, I guess, I became convinced that people really need to act as kind of support mechanisms for each other. Maybe I've let it become a little exaggerated.

A: Still, you know, I don't think you can blame yourself for your mother's illness. It was unforgivable of her.

B: Please don't criticize my mother.

A: I can't believe you're defending her. After the guilt she made you feel.

B: I don't feel guilty, I feel sorry.

A: It certainly made you overdependent on other people, that's for sure.

B: Either that, or I depend on the wrong people.

A: What does that mean?

B: Well, maybe you're a little self-absorbed.

A: What?

B: A bit unwilling to give, you know? To reach out and share other people's lives.

A: I don't think that's true at all.

B: No?

A: No. I admit I enjoy freedom, but . . .

B: I know, I've heard it all before. I guess I've known a lot of very selfish people.

A: I don't think it's selfish to ask for a little time for myself. I don't know why it is, but I seem to attract very demanding people. Every time I get to know somebody, they always seem to turn out to be the kind of person who can't stand on their own two feet. I've never been able to understand why people can't be left alone for five minutes.

B: Invading your personal space, right?

A: You make it sound frivolous.

B: No, no. You just might wake up one day and find yourself without friends, that's all.

A: I'll take that chance.

B: Fine.

A: It's time to go in.

B: Yes.

A: I'll be right back.

B: Where are you going?

——————— • • • ———————

Scenes for Three Actors

SCENE 25

• •

The addition of the third actor complicates the construction of character: focus is more diffuse and **motivational units** sometimes alternate more rapidly from one focus point to another. The balance of power in this scene switches back and forth among the three characters, and so does the focus. Investigate the past history of the characters—hints are given in the text—in determining such traits as patience, tolerance, and egocentricity. The environment can, perhaps, be blamed for frayed tempers, but the ethics and social training of the characters are equally significant and will vary depending on how you develop them. Don't substitute stereotypes for in-depth characterization.

A: Next, please.

B: That's me.

A: Yes.

B: Finally.

A: Excuse me?

B: It's been a while.

A: Has it?

B: I've been waiting for more than an hour.

A: Have you?

B: I'm not complaining, of course.

A: No.

B: But it has been a while.

A: I see. Now then, what is your name?

C: I'm sorry for interrupting, but could you tell me . . . do you have any idea how long it's going to be?

A: In a hurry?

C: Well, I do have another appointment in about thirty minutes.

B: Me, too.

A: I'm afraid I can't tell you how . . .

C: Don't I know you from somewhere?

A: Me? Personal conversation is not allowed here, and . . .

C: No, no. You.

B: Me?

C: Yes. Didn't we . . .

B: Oh, right?

C: Ann Arbor, right?

B: Sure! I remember you!

C: That workshop in social activism.

A: I'd like to call to your attention that you're breaking several rules by this conversation. Do you suppose we could . . .

B: Absolutely. 1968, wasn't it?

A: Could we get on with this?

C: 1967.

B: Was it?

C: Yeah. Bobby was still alive.

A: The line is backing up.

B: Oh, right. Did you work for Bobby?

A: And I have a lot of paperwork to do.

C: Of course. How are you?

B: Fine. You?

A: So if we could . . .

C: Such a long time.

B: Yes. More than twenty years.

A: Look, I'm going to have to ask you . . .

C: Twenty years!

A: Would you go back to your place, please?

C: And you haven't changed a bit!

B: You think so?

A: Please go back to your place.

C: Not a bit.

A: Social responsibility makes it imperative that . . .

B: Well, I have, you know. Changed.

A: . . . that we proceed with . . .

C: No, no.

A: This interview must continue!

B: Inside, I mean.

C: Oh, well . . .

A: You must be quiet and allow proper procedure or I'll get the supervisor over here!

C: That's not very nice.

A: Well, you're not very nice, either.

C: What?

A: Interfering with the process this way. Not very nice.

C: I'm not interfering. I'm interacting.

B: Maybe we should talk later.

C: I'm operating on a very positive level here.

A: You're interfering.

B: We could go have a cup of coffee as soon as this is over, okay?

A: And interference cannot be tolerated. Now go away.

C: You're responding to me in a fascist manner. Bossing me around. I hate being bossed around.

B: I'll meet you down at the corner in about fifteen minutes, all right?

A: If you hate being instructed in proper behavior, then you don't belong here.

C: Oh, really?

A: That's right. So you might as well go.

B: For now, anyway.

A: For good.

C: Fine. I certainly don't want to be here. I really don't like your attitude at all. You should not be in charge of a social institution like this. You should not be responsible for other people. You are unfair.

A: That is your opinion. And your opinion isn't important.

C: Oh?

A: No. You have no knowledge of this institution and are trying to impose your will out of ignorance. So I have decided that you would never fit in here. I want you to leave. Now.

B: There really isn't any need for this, you know. We could all be friends, but we have to cool down first.

A: Or I'll call the guards.

C: I'm going to leave. You know I have no choice. But someday you're going to realize what a bully you are and wish you had been more sensitive and receptive. I could have been a force for fruitful change around here. But you'll never know, will you?

A: I don't suppose I will.

C: The next time you see me, you'll realize that you made a bad mistake here today.

A: Is that a threat?

B: Please don't shout.

C: And you. You're lending your presence to a restrictive and bureaucratic machine. How could you?

B: I just don't like to see people lose their tempers and become violent. I just want people to be nice to each other.

C: At no matter what cost? That's collaboration.

B: Well, maybe I'm not as dedicated as you are. Or as I used to be.

C: Obviously not.

B: Wait . . .

A: Now then, back to important matters. What's your name?

B: I'm not staying.

A: Oh?

B: No. My friend was right. I've gotten weak over the years. I don't want to be where people are treated the way you treated my friend. I'm tempted to report you to your superior for rude, overbearing behavior.

A: Just doing my job.

B: Oh. Right. Good-bye.

A: Good-bye. Next.

SCENE 26

• •

Three very different attitudes are expressed by the characters here, each of whom undergoes a major transition during the scene. Their situation is purposely obscure and complex, requiring you to use considerable imagination in determining the activity in which they are involved. Spend some time creating environment and allow the personal characteristics to evolve from it. The scene also offers an excellent opportunity to practice **sense memory** skills.

A: Red.

B: You think so?

C: Or blue.

A: No, no . . .

B: Green?

C: Yellow, maybe.

A: Oh, now it's a mess.

B: Of course it isn't.

C: Well . . .

A: And it's going to fall over.

B: We can fix that.

C: Can we?

A: How?

B: Go get some wire.

C: Wire?

A: We're all out.

B: Buy some more.

C: Where?

A: All the stores are closed.

B: We'll think of something.

C: I wonder if . . .

A: I think it's going to rain.

B: That's okay.

C: Is it?

A: Yes. Look over there.

B: That's nothing.

C: Are you sure?

A: Looks pretty bad to me.

B: I've got an idea!

C: I think the wind's picking up, too.

A: Probably.

B: If we take this and put it over there . . .

C: Didn't we try that once before?

A: I'm sure we did.

B: No, no. Look . . . see? Oh . . .

C: What?

A: I told you.

B: It was worth a try.

C: Maybe we should just start over again.

A: I couldn't bear that.

B: I don't think we need to start over.

C: But I'm not even certain of the concept.

A: I'm sick of the whole thing.

B: How about this?

C: What are you doing?

A: Don't do that!

B: No, look . . .

C: What was that noise?

A: Now you've done it.

B: It's doing something anyway.

C: Yeah. But what?

A: Moving, for one thing.

B: Toward us . . .

C: Get out of the way!

A: We're going to die!

B: Run!

C: Which way?

A: Look!

B: It's stopping!

C: Is it?

A: Yes!

B: It's stopped.

C: What happened?

A: Boy, was I scared!

B: I'm still scared.

C: I wasn't scared.

A: That was kind of interesting, though.

B: You think so?

C: Definitely.

A: You know, I think that might be the answer.

B: What do you mean? It fell apart.

C: Not really.

A: Maybe it's supposed to move like that.

B: No way.

C: You're right.

A: And the mistake we made was thinking about color too early.

B: The whole thing is a mistake.

C: We can market this, you know.

A: Yes!

B: Who would want it?

C: Everybody who lives in small, cramped apartments.

A: Think of the money we'd make. Millions.

B: Dreamer.

C: Pick up that end.

A: Set it down gently.

B: Why bother?

C: Now hand me that.

A: Which?

B: The red one.

C: No, the blue one.

A: Maybe yellow?

B: Or blue?

A: Get a firm grip now.

C: I am.

A: Watch out!

B: Help!

C: Look at it go!

A: Can we catch it?

B: No.

C: Yes!

A: Amazing.

B: Now it's really lost.

C: No! Here it comes again!

A: Is that it?

B: Absolutely!

C: Watch out!

SCENE 27

• •

This scene is based on memory. The relationship between the three characters could be that of siblings, or they could be friends; in any event, they share a close bond. As the characterizations can be very complex, care must be taken in making subtextual choices. Especially helpful here would be detailed birth-to-death characterizational biographies, which the three actors read and discuss among themselves. Explore ways in which the emotional climate of the scene affects the pace and rhythm of the build. Watch for the big transition that occurs before the appearance of the photograph.

A: Do you remember Joe Grant?

B: Who's Joe Grant?

A: My high-school biology teacher.

B: How could I remember your high-school biology teacher?

A: I don't know, I just thought . . .

C: I remember him.

A: Do you?

C: Yeah. Barely.

B: I wasn't even born when you were in high school.

A: Really?

B: Really. I wasn't born when you were in college.

C: I was. I remember Mom took me to your high-school graduation and this guy came up and threw me in the air.

A: That was Joe Grant.

C: Yeah. Scared me to death.

B: I guess he was dead by the time I came along.

A: Oh, no. He moved away.

C: Where to?

A: Alaska, I think.

C: Good place for him.

B: Cool him down. Sounds like a jerk.

C: No. Just big and primitive.

B: Huh! A real swell guy.

A: He was.

C: If you like the type.

A: I guess I did. Sort of direct and honest.

C: Yeah. Throwing people around.

B: I remember you being pretty rough on me, as a matter of fact.

C: Me?

B: No, not you.

A: Not me.

B: Yeah. You.

A: What did I ever do to you?

B: You locked me in the attic a couple of times.

A: I never.

C: Yes, you did. I helped you once.

B: And nobody came to let me out until supper time. I thought I was going to die.

A: Oh, come on.

B: It was summertime and it must have been 120 degrees in that attic by the middle of the afternoon. I cried so much I dehydrated.

A: You exaggerate everything.

C: It was a pretty awful thing to do.

B: And you hung me up by my heels in the grape arbor once.

A: You're imagining things.

B: I think that's why I have back problems to this day.

A: You make me sound like an ogre.

B: You certainly caused me a lot of pain. To this day.

C: Well . . .

B: What?

C: Nothing.

B: Come on. What?

C: I was just going to say . . . oh, never mind. You'll just get mad.

B: Whatever it is, you've got to say it now.

C: It's just that you always have been a kind of . . . well, a hypochondriac.

B: You're a rotten liar.

C: I told you you'd get mad.

B: It's not true, you creep.

A: Come on, you two . . .

C: Who are you calling a creep?

A: Settle down, now.

B: Don't tell us what to do.

C: Yeah.

A: Fine. I was just . . .

B: You have dedicated your life to bossing us around, and I'm sick of it.

C: Me, too.

A: Well, if you'd stop acting like children, then I wouldn't have to, would I?

B: We are not children.

C: Absolutely not.

A: I didn't say you were children. I said you acted like children.

B: Oh, you're just impossible.

A: I don't want to talk about this anymore.

B: Fine.

C: As usual.

A: Look at this.

B: What is it?

A: It's us.

C: What? Let me see?

A: Don't grab.

C: Look at us.

B: Where was that taken?

A: Silver Lake.

B: Really?

C: Sure. Oh, look at my Huckleberry Hound T-shirt.

A: Look at your nose.

B: Always sunburned.

C: I couldn't help it. I have sensitive skin.

B: Hypochondriac.

A: Those were the days, weren't they?

B: Oh, yeah.

C: Summer.

A: Silver Lake.

B: Pineapple-grapefruit juice.

C: Twinkies.

B: Finally being able to swim out to the diving platform.

A: You were never able to swim out to the diving platform.

B: I was, too.

A: Not when I was there.

C: Long time ago.

B: Yeah.

A: Those were the days . . .

B: Yeah.

C: Oh, yeah.

A: They'll never come again.

B: No . . .

C: No . . .

SECTION THREE
• • • •
FINDING RHYTHM: PACE AND RATE

You know the play—its conflicts, the rise and fall of its actions, its message to the world. You know the character, the details of another life from birth to death—joys and anxieties, anger and laughter. Now: How do you get all this across to the audience who has gathered to receive your performance? Well, one of the ways is by understanding the rhythm of the character, the scene, the play. A good play, like an hour or two of your own life, contains a variety of rhythms. Time passes swiftly or slowly. You're in a listening mood or an aggressively articulate one. You interrupt or are interrupted. You allow your thoughts to trail off lazily or in confusion or boredom. You search for the right words to express your thoughts, move quickly from idea to idea, or pause while you choose the right word. Think of all these rhythms when you work on these scenes. The scene needs as much variety as real life does.

Scenes for Two Actors

SCENE 28

• •

This scene is very fast-paced, providing an excellent opportunity to practice overlapping dialogue (**dovetailing** or **telescoping**). Especially difficult in such a scene is motivating the many short pauses required of one character so that the other character's dialogue can be inserted between the first character's words as the scene progresses. Remember that not only must the other character's words be heard, but there must be a legitimate and logical reason for the hesitation that allows them to be heard. There are also several words that may be—and perhaps should be—spoken simultaneously. Also watch out for normally paced interrupts and trail-offs. Remember: These techniques of pace and rhythm are designed to allow the characters' conversation to sound more realistic. Their lines should never sound stylized or artificial, as if they were drawn from an Ionesco play.

A: Okay, now here's the idea . . .

B: I can't do this.

A: You go in first and get to this point . . .

B: No.

A: . . . then I come in and get to here. Then you . . .

B: I'm afraid.

A: . . . take it from there.

B: You're not listening to me.

A: After that, it'll be very easy. All we have to do is . . .

B: I'm leaving.

A: . . . pick up the last pieces and get out. Where are you going?

B: Home.

A: Of course you're not going home. We have . . .

B: Oh, yes I am. I've been telling you over . . .

A: . . . work to do. Now sit down and . . .

B: . . . and over again. That I can't . . .

A: . . . listen to what I have to say. Time is limited and . . .

B: . . . do this. I'm just not cut out for . . .

A: . . . if we waste any more of it we're never going to . . .

B: . . . this kind of activity. I'm just not . . .

A: . . . get through this. Now tell me again . . .

B: . . . strong enough. I really think you're going to have . . .

A: . . . what you have to do. Come on, do it or I'll have . . .

B: . . . to find somebody else.

A: . . . to find somebody else.

B: I'm sorry.

A: What for?

B: I . . .

A: Nothing to be sorry for.

B: I feel a lot of guilt. Do you think you can . . .

A: We do what we can.

B: . . . forgive me? I know you've been . . .

A: You can't help being weak.

B: . . . counting on me. But there doesn't . . .

A: Born that way, I guess.

B: . . . seem to be anything I can do about it. What can I . . .

A: Some people have it, some people don't.

B: . . . say. I . . .

A: And you just don't.

B: . . . wish I could live up to your . . .

A: I'm sorry I built up such high . . .

B: . . . expectations.

A: . . . expectations.

B: What did you . . .

A: Huh?

B: . . . say?

A: Nothing. Go on . . .

B: About . . .

A: . . . home.

B: . . . expectations?

A: Just that I was sorry . . .

B: You still . . .

A: . . . I had any.

B: . . . have any?

A: Of you?

B: Of me?

A: No.

B: No?

A: The question is . . .

B: I don't know why I'm surprised. I don't really . . .

A: . . . do you have any . . .

B: . . . have any . . .

A: . . . of yourself?

B: . . . of myself.

A: That's the thing. That's the question . . .

B: And the answer is . . .

A: . . . you have to ask yourself.

B: . . . I don't know.

A: You don't?

B: No.

A: Well . . .

B: Good-bye, then . . .

A: Good-bye. I'll . . .

B: . . . I guess.

A: . . . see you around.

B: Yeah.

SCENE 29

• •

The long speeches in this scene give it a rhythm that is the complete opposite of the preceding one. It is a slow-paced, probing sort of scene in which it will be very important for you to listen intently to what is being said, and not only to what the other character is saying—you're going to have to listen more intently than usual to what your own character is saying. This **listening** process is unusually important in a scene like this one because it is the only way to find the pauses, and finding pauses (there are places for many) and finding their length (they can often be quite long) is essential to the truth of the scene. One of the characters seems to be operating at a higher emotional level, which means honesty of thought and effective delivery are of great importance and their absence glaringly obvious. The other character tends to be more objective and low-key; making the speech interesting and vivid is one of the tasks in such a case. Because maintaining energy in a slow-paced scene can be difficult, the actors may have to work harder than is immediately apparent. Find a true motivation for the very unexpected last line; it should not come simply from irrational or aberrant emotion. Remember: Listening is as important (and as active) as speaking.

A: It all began a couple of weeks ago. That's when I decided I had to change psychiatrists. A very important and delicate move, of course. I knew that, but I felt it was absolutely necessary.

B: Why?

A: Oh, many reasons. First of all, the doctor I was seeing was a complete fanatic as far as drugs were concerned. I mean, her solution to any problem that came up was to give me a prescription. That's how I got hooked. I wasn't even aware of how dangerous those kinds of drugs could be. I just took whatever she prescribed for me—just accepted whatever it was without question. Like an idiot. You know what I mean?

B: Yes.

A: Well, so, that was the main thing. But also, I gradually began to realize that she was pretty insensitive to some of my other problems.

B: Such as?

A: I was getting to be very withdrawn, and I didn't even realize it. I never went anywhere, never did anything, never saw anyone. I was completely isolated and alienated. Totally unable to relate to anyone. Not that there was anyone to relate to. You know? What's that called?

B: Agoraphobia.

A: Yeah. Right. So days would go by and I never left my apartment. I set up this system, see, so that everything I needed, like groceries and stuff, would be delivered to my front door. Never needed to go out, see. Just to see the shrink once a week and even then I'd call a cab to come to the front door and have it take me to the doctor's front door. Finally it got to be weeks. One morning I woke up and I realized that it had been over a month since I'd been outside. The psychiatrist was on vacation, see, so I hadn't even been outside to see her.

B: Uh-huh.

A: Well, so the next day was my first appointment with her since she came back from her vacation, and when I got there, the first thing I said to her was that I thought I was getting really withdrawn, and you know what she said?

B: What?

A: She said: "Well, you ought to get out more." Then she gave me a new prescription. You believe that? Isn't that absolutely incredible?

B: Well . . .

A: So that was when I knew I had to change shrinks.

B: I see.

A: So. Aren't you going to react?

B: What do you want me to say?

A: Gosh, I don't know. That's your job, isn't it? To say the right thing?

B: You want answers, is that it?

A: Well, yes. I do.

B: How long have you been in therapy?

A: Seven years. Going on eight.

B: Then you should know by now that the real answers are not going to come from me, but from inside yourself.

A: Yes, but . . .

B: First of all, let's get a couple of things clear. Are you still taking the drugs you told me about?

A: Yes.

B: Do you want to stop?

A: Well . . .

B: Do you realize such drugs can actively and strongly contribute to your agoraphobia? That they may, in fact, be the sole and only activating factor for your alienation and isolation? Did you know that such conditions are often chemically created and almost always chemically sustained? Often by doctors and practitioners who may or may not be honorably motivated. Did you know that?

A: No.

B: Well, it's true. So it would seem to me that the first thing you have to do is stop taking the drugs. And in order to do that, you must want to stop taking them. What do you think? Are you not sure of the answer or do you know the answer but are afraid to tell me?

A: I don't know.

B: Are you often depressed? Do you sometimes contemplate suicide? Do you have unexplained skin irritations? Itching?

A: Yes . . .

B: All of those things or some of them?

A: All of them.

B: So it seems important to me that you discontinue the drugs. But you must come to that decision yourself. How can I help you to do that? If you are unable to do so today, perhaps next time we can . . .

A: No. I've decided.

B: Are you sure?

A: Yes. I'll quit. I'll stop today. I'll never take another one.

B: I'm afraid it isn't that easy. You cannot stop taking these drugs abruptly. Absolutely not. You must let the drugs leave your body gradually. To do otherwise is to risk serious damage, both mentally and physically. I will provide you with a phased schedule that you must follow in freeing yourself from this addiction, and you must adhere to it strictly. This is very important and I must have your complete and unqualified cooperation, otherwise we can't work together. Do you understand?

A: Yes.

B: As the drugs leave your body, you must force yourself to go out into the city on an increasing basis. Assign yourself tasks which require you to leave your apartment. Stick to short, nonstressful excursions at first. Walk to the corner grocery store, for instance. As you become drug-free, I believe the fear of social interaction will decrease. In the meantime, I'll need to see you three times a week. All right?

A: Yes.

B: Anything you want to say?

A: Well . . .

B: Yes?

A: I love you.

SCENE 30

• •

This scene is specifically designed to provide exercise in building a scene in which the most important rhythmic feature is the pause. The situation seems clear: family members holding vigil over a relative who appears to be terminally ill. The time is definite: the scene begins at two o'clock and ends at five after. It may come as a surprise to see how difficult it is to make the scene last as long as five minutes. Keep at it. Fill the pauses with thought, constructing subtext that will take the characters from one motivational unit to the next without strain and with properly motivated silences.

A: What time is it?

B: Two o'clock.

A: I keep falling asleep.

B: Me, too.

A: I remember when he took us to the river. To that big sandbar. All those rocks. We'd spend all day there.

B: Great place to catch tadpoles.

A: Yeah. In mason jars.

B: Long time ago.

A: Yes.

B: I'm so sleepy.

A: Yes.

B: What was that?

A: What?

B: I thought . . .

A: Is he all right?

B: Yes . . .

A: Every little noise . . .

B: I know . . .

A: How do other people cope with this?

B: I don't know.

A: For so long . . .

B: How long has it been?

A: I don't know. Too long.

B: I spoke to Aunt Mildred today.

A: What did she want?

B: Well, she wanted to know if we had made any . . . arrangements.

A: She would.

B: She meant well. I told her that we hadn't, but that he had.

A: Has he?

B: He told me about a year ago that he'd joined a . . . I guess it's called a . . . society. They . . . take care of everything. All we have to do is call them when . . .

A: . . . yes.

B: And they'll come and . . . take care of everything.

A: Well . . . good.

B: I suppose.

A: What time is it?

B: Just after two.

A: I don't know how much longer I can . . .

B: Nice night.

A: Yes.

B: So still . . .

A: When will you go back?

B: Oh, I don't know . . .

A: So much depends on . . .

B: Yes.

A: It can't be too much longer.

B: You wouldn't think so.

A: No . . .

B: It's very difficult.

A: Oh, yes.

B: Just us . . .

A: Hmmm?

B: It'll be just us.

A: Well . . .

B: From now on . . .

A: Kind of . . .

B: Just us . . .

A: Kind of . . . diminished . . .

B: Yes . . .

A: It happens, I suppose.

B: Happens to everybody.

A: What time is it?

B: Five after two.

SCENE 31

• •

Here is a scene in which the rhythm is deliberately out of balance. In the beginning, one of the characters expresses urgency in fast-paced, short bursts, while the other reminisces at a much more leisurely pace. Gradually, the rhythm of the scene reverses itself, and then reverses itself again. The problems in such a scene are: How does the fast-paced character maintain the quickness and sense of urgency in the face of the other's slow meditativeness? How is panic or fear maintained silently? Also, a switch occurs from one **circle of concentration** to another—from intense awareness of the immediate (rather critical) situation, to a kind of daydream or fantasy. This kind of transition can be difficult. Be sure your subtextual thought pattern is strong so that the switch in concentration focus can be effectively made.

A: Come on! Let's go!

B: Are you sure you want to do this? I think maybe it would be better if we waited a while, you know? I mean, this could really be dangerous, and my horoscope in the paper this morning told me to be careful. So don't you think . . . how did I get this dirt on my hands?

A: No, no! Come on! Hurry up!

B: I haven't been handling anything that was dirty. Not that I can remember. Now let me think . . . no, nothing that I can think of. I did read the newspaper, but it doesn't look like that black stuff— ink, I guess—that rubs off of newspapers, does it? Do you think it does?

A: Look over there!

B: Where? I'm really hungry, you know? Do you think we could find someplace to eat? I don't think I've had anything to eat today. Not since breakfast, anyway.

A: Get your head down!

B: Of course, it was a pretty heavy breakfast. Let's see, what did I have? Eggs, bacon, toast, jelly, butter, orange juice, milk, and coffee . . .

A: Watch out!

B: . . . a waffle, syrup, an English muffin, half a pineapple, and a honeydew melon. And some salsa. With a tortilla.

A: Okay, now we can leave. All clear. Come to think of it, I'm kind of hungry, too. Where is it you want to go exactly?

B: Anywhere else. Away from here. It's nearly three o'clock. Come on, let's go.

A: What are you talking about? This neighborhood isn't all that bad. Most of the time. We just hit a bad day. Of course, I know there're some pretty rough types that hang around here, but I don't think they wake up until later.

B: Oh, yeah? Who are those guys over there?

A: Behind those ruins, you mean? Gee, I don't know. Why do you suppose they're smoking like that? Do you think they could've been blown up or something? And if they were, why were they? I mean it really does look like a perfectly peaceful place except for that. At least at this time of the day it does. Later on, of course . . .

B: I don't think it looks peaceful! Those guys . . .

A: Later on, I expect, it isn't so safe. Are you scared? I don't think there's anything to be scared of.

B: Oh, no? What do you think they want, then?

A: I don't know. Probably just want to borrow a match or something. Hey, there's a restaurant right here. Why don't we just go in and . . . oh, the door's locked. Do you think it's closed? Oh, look at those people coming this way. Do you think they're friends with those guys over by the ruins? They must be, they're making signs of some kind to them.

B: I'm scared! Let's go!

A: It always intrigues me to try and figure out what relationship people have to each other. Doesn't that interest you? I mean, complete strangers can be fascinating . . .

B: I'll think of something else, take my mind off all this. What'll I think about?

A: On the other hand, sometimes strangers can just be threatening.

B: I'll think about London in the spring: one of those warm spring days they get over there sometimes, with chestnut trees in bloom.

A: Hey! That guy has a gun! The one in front!

B: I'll pretend I'm walking along the Thames by Waterloo Bridge, browsing in the bookseller's stalls. People sitting around on the benches, taking in the sun. Everybody having a good time, everybody relaxing . . .

A: My God! They all have guns!

B: And over there's Big Ben and the Houses of Parliament. What time does it say? Six o'clock?

A: What are we going to do?

B: It'll be dark pretty soon.

A: We're going to be killed!

B: It's late . . .

A: Let's get out of here!

B: Too late!

SCENE 32

• •

This scene concentrates on the two types of fragmented speech that occur most often: the interrupt and the trail-off. It's your task to decide which of the lines need to be interrupted by the other character and which are to be treated as incomplete thoughts in which the speaker allows his or her speech to trail off into silence. Many of the lines could be interpreted either way. Subtext and **line reading**, of course, change radically depending on which decision is made, as does rhythm.

A: I wonder . . .

B: What?

A: Do you think I could find . . .

B: Listen!

A: What?

B: No, never mind. I thought . . .

A: If I went over that way, I'll bet I could find a way out of here.

B: Isn't that the way we came in? It seems to me . . .

A: That's the way we came in. Over there . . .

B: Is it? Wasn't there . . . no, maybe you're right . . .

A: I'm sure of it. I remember we passed that . . .

B: There it is again!

A: What do you hear?

B: Well, it sounds like . . .

A: What? What?

B: Some kind of . . .

A: Oh, yes. I hear it now. Like a . . .

B: Band. A marching . . .

A: Band. Yes.

B: But surely . . .

A: There wouldn't be a . . .

B: No.

A: Not around here.

B: Unless, maybe, there was a small high school around here somewhere. They might have a band. And they might be, you know, rehearsing or . . .

A: Not very likely, do you think?

B: Well . . .

A: Not impossible, of course. Not . . .

B: No.

A: Not totally out of the question.

B: Oh, no.

A: On the other hand . . .

B: Yes?

A: Maybe we're hearing things. Maybe we're . . .

B: I don't think so.

A: No?

B: I've never had an aural hallucination . . .

A: A what?

B: . . . in my life.

A: I wasn't . . .

B: Or have I? Let me think . . .

A: That's not what I meant. I just . . .

B: No. I'm quite sure I haven't.

A: I thought maybe it was another sound that we were mistaking for the sound of a band. Not that we were . . .

B: Like what?

A: Pardon?

B: Like what other kind of sound? What sounds like a . . .

A: Oh, I don't know. Crickets, maybe, or . . .

B: Crickets?

A: Well . . . or frogs . . .

B: Frogs?

A: It was just a thought . . .

B: No, I think it was a real marching band. I certainly don't think it was . . .

A: Listen!

B: Over there!

A: Look!

B: What in the world . . .

A: I . . .

B: Watch out for the . . .

SCENE 33

• •

How does physical activity influence the pace and rhythm of a scene? Be aware that any kind of movement is going to take time and must be an organic part of the overall timing of the scene. Here we have an example of two people operating some kind of apparatus—what sort is relatively unimportant, but fun to create—and the activity itself interrupts the action, causes pauses, and finally sets the pace. The scene is an excellent opportunity to work on sense memory, and the ending can give free rein to **emotion memory** as well.

A: Careful . . .

B: Pick up that . . .

A: I am, but . . .

B: Okay, now . . .

A: One, two, three . . .

B: Up!

A: There.

B: Good.

A: I never thought we'd make that.

B: More to come.

A: I know.

B: Here we go . . .

A: Start it up.

B: Go!

A: That's too fast!

B: Okay, okay . . .

A: Wait a minute . . .

B: Better?

A: I think so . . .

B: Quick . . .

A: I'm going as fast as . . .

B: Well, you'll have to go . . .

A: Slow it down!

B: Faster!

A: I can't . . .

B: Catch it!

A: Wait!

B: Watch out!

A: I told you it was too fast.

B: What was I supposed to do?

A: Go faster, that's what you were supposed to do.

B: Not physically possible.

A: Well, if I slow it down, it won't work as well.

B: Try it and see.

A: We'll never . . .

B: Try it and see!

A: Okay, here goes . . .

B: Too fast . . . slower . . . slower . . .

A: That'll never . . .

B: It will! It will! Watch!

A: If I . . .

B: Yes! Now . . .

A: Come over here, now . . .

B: Match it up, now . . . careful!

A: Are you all right?

B: Yes! Easy now . . .

A: Here we go . . .

B: Easy, easy . . .

A: I think . . .

B: Here we . . .

A: We're going to . . .

B: Go . . .

A: . . . make it!

B: I think so.

A: There!

B: Now all we have to do is fasten this.

A: No, we have to slide this in first.

B: Do we?

A: Of course.

B: How does it attach?

A: Through here.

B: Okay, here it . . .

A: Let me . . .

B: . . . comes.

A: . . . have it.

B: Good.

A: Now then . . .

B: Ready?

A: Yes.

B: Turn it on!

A: There!

B: Look at that!

A: I can't believe it!

B: It's working!

A: Watch out!

B: It's out of control!

A: Get out of the way!

B: Duck!

A: I . . .

B: Are you all right? I said, are you all right? Hey . . . say something . . . hey . . .

SCENE 34

• •

Here the pace problem is delineated by the split focus. At what rate would a nearly automatic task be conducted as opposed to a personal, free-wheeling conversation? Do the two rates tend to overlap and/or influence each other? What about pace? Is there significant pause time between the job and the conversation? Or does the repetitive nature of the job allow for transition to personal speech more quickly than might be expected? The job itself is obviously something akin to ushering or ticket taking, though you are certainly free to imagine an entirely different task. Whatever your decision, the scene exercises sense memory to some extent. The job the characters are doing will involve a good many physical actions; make sure they are accurately created and executed. The theater patrons' (or other kinds of customers') remarks are obviously heard only by the actors, so allow for listening time when appropriate.

A: We have been trying to get away for ages now, and it finally looks as if we're going to be able to do it. Probably some time in . . . that'll be three dollars and seventy-five cents, please. Thank you.

B: This way, please. Turn to the left . . . sometime in when? Did you say?

A: In August, I think. That's what we're aiming for at any rate.

B: I'm sorry, I can't change a bill that size. Do you have anything smaller?

A: Of course, who knows? It may be September . . . this way, please. Upstairs on the left . . . maybe never.

B: I know what you mean . . . three dollars seventy-five, please. Thank you. But it'll happen. Someday.

A: Hold that thought . . . I'm sorry, I'm not able to take a twenty-dollar bill. Do you have anything smaller? Thank you . . . I'll tell you one thing, though. I have got to get out of here. I think if I have to fight the traffic to get to work much longer I'll go nuts.

B: Upstairs on your right . . . I know. How far is your commute?

A: Over an hour. Isn't that outrageous? Not to mention that the car I drive . . . I'm sorry, sir, but cameras are not allowed. Thank you . . . the car I drive is over ten years old and about as dependable as the Easter Bunny.

B: Thank you. Twenty-five cents is your change . . . I always thought the Easter Bunny was pretty reliable.

A: Very funny . . . yes, madam, the women's rest room is down the stairs and to your right . . . you know what I mean.

B: Well, he always left me chocolate eggs, that's all I can say.

A: No, madam, to your right. Yes. That's right . . . never missed an Easter, huh?

B: Never . . . watch out, sir, mind your step . . . not to this day.

A: You got chocolate eggs last Easter? At your age?

B: What do you mean, my age?

A: Approximately ten thirty-five, sir, unless there is an unexpected delay. Well, I'm sorry, sir, but we can't be more exact than that. Delays do happen, and sometimes we have no control over them. Yes, sir. Sorry, sir. Up the stairs and to your right. No, sir, up the stairs. The rest rooms are downstairs . . . honestly, who do they think we are? I can only give out the information that I have . . . no, sir, the men's room is on the left.

B: Thank you . . . what do you mean, my age?

A: Oh, don't be so sensitive. You know what I mean.

B: Actually, I don't . . . about eight o'clock, sir. No, sir, we do not expect to be late tonight, but circumstances beyond our control sometimes . . . well, how rude.

A: Aren't they all? Aren't they all?

B: I don't think I'm particularly sensitive, by the way. Not about my age. Not overly sensitive.

A: Thank you for telling me, sir. I'll get someone to take care of it . . . he wants me to replace the toilet paper myself, right?

B: Right. They expect everything.

A: Three dollars and seventy-five cents, please. Thank you. Your change is one dollar and twenty-five cents. Mind your step, please . . . I know they do, and I'm very tired of it.

B: I'm thinking of going back to school . . . downstairs and to the right, madam . . . that's how tired I am of it.

A: You try to go to school and do this at the same time and you'll really be tired.

B: But I'll be training to do something else. I'll have some hope. That's the point.

A: Here comes a rush.

B: Thank you, sir. Here's your change . . . twenty-five cents . . .

A: I'm sorry, I can't accept a twenty-dollar bill, do you have anything smaller? Yes, of course you can complain to the manager. The office is across the hall. Thank you . . . what a jerk . . . downstairs on your right, madam.

B: Thank you, miss . . . we should start a jerk count . . . promptly at eight o'clock, sir, as far as we know. Unless there is an unexpected delay.

A: Approximately ten thirty-five, madam, unless there is a delay over which we have no control. Thank you, sir.

B: Your change is one dollar and twenty-five cents, madam. Thank you . . . oh, when will this be over? Thank you, sir.

A: No . . . upstairs and to your left. Thank you.

B: Promptly at eight o'clock, sir, unless . . . same to you. Thank you . . . beginning to thin out, now . . .

A: Not thin enough . . . thank you, madam . . .

B: There! That's that!

A: You think so?

B: For now, at least.

A: Going back to school, huh?

B: Yeah.

A: Little old for that, aren't you?

B: Downstairs on your left, sir . . . what does that mean?

SCENE 35

• •

The situation in this scene reverses the usual speech ratio of rate to length. The character with the longer lines is forced by the situation to speak faster than the character with the shorter lines. The ratio changes from character to character toward the end of the scene. How does this unusual circumstance affect motivation? How does the character who is forced to speak rapidly motivate silence while the slow-speaking character talks? The plot allows for imaginative establishment of environment and for plenty of sense-memory exercise.

A: All right, now, listen carefully because I don't have very much time. I have to get back on the job before anyone misses me, and it's very important that you remember everything I have to say. Do you understand?

B: Just a minute, okay . . . I have something in my shoe . . . I think it's a . . . no, it isn't . . .

A: Never mind what you have in your shoe, okay? You've got to be very alert and completely clear on what I have to say. Here's the deal. You go over to that pay phone over there, the one by the library, and dial this number. Here, take it.

B: Hold on for a . . . I can't get my finger out of . . .

A: Take this number!

B: . . . Okay.

A: When the time comes, now, I want you to dial that number and say to whoever answers that you have to speak to me. Tell them it's a family emergency. Tell them that my grandmother is dying and that you have to talk to me right away. Wait a minute, wait a minute, somebody's coming over here and I can't let them see me. Get out of my way!

B: Where? I don't see anybody . . . oh, over there, you mean? I think that's just the . . . isn't that the ice-cream man? Should I get an ice cream, do you think? Or should I . . .

A: Get down, get down! Don't you know anything? Don't you know that an ice-cream man is their favorite form of cover? Where did you get your training, anyway? How come you're so stupid and waste so much time?

B: Now, just a minute, here . . . I'm not stupid . . . and I don't see why you're in such a hurry . . . I think . . .

A: Look, it really doesn't matter what you think, does it? The important thing is that we get done what we have to get done and in order to do that we have to hurry. Now, the person you'll get on the line will be giving you information on getting into the house, where to find the key, stuff like that.

B: Gosh, I really have . . . I have this terrific headache, you know? I can't seem . . . to concentrate on anything . . . do you think I should rest for a while?

A: No! Now try to pay attention. Think you can do that?

B: Oh, look . . . over there . . . he's coming this way . . .

A: Watch out!

B: Oh!

A: Get out of the . . .

B: Are you all right?

A: I think I'm . . . I don't . . . how did he . . .

B: Here, let me do that. No, no, stop moving around like that. He's over there behind those bushes, I think, and if we don't do something pretty quick he's going to start again.

A: Oh . . .

B: Here, quick, take this handkerchief and hold it to your . . .

A: . . . thanks . . . I'm . . . I can't . . .

B: You'll be fine. But we have to move fast. There! He's going. He's running down toward the lake. He must have a boat down there. Okay, quick now, stand up. We've got to get out of here.

A: You go on . . . there's no way I can . . . you go . . .

B: Not a chance. I'm not just going to leave you here. But we have to move. Trouble is, I don't think I can carry you. Can I?

A: No . . . you . . . can't . . .

B: All right, then. Think! Think of something to do! We've got to really move before . . . look, there's another one. And he really is moving fast. We have to do something and we have to be quick!

A: Go . . . get out of here . . . just . . . leave . . .

B: Here. Get over here and lie as close to this as you can. I'm going to cover you with this and then all you have to do is lie still and not move. I'm going for help. You got all that? Hey! There's no time! Did you hear me? Hey!

SCENE 36

• •

This scene provides the acting student with an exercise in pacing the monologue and a good deal of opportunity to develop skills in listening. Realize that one of the ways to keep long speeches interesting is rhythmic variety. Find places in the speeches when fast rate is motivated by the thought pattern, then contrast these moments with the long, reflective pauses that such "memory" speeches so effectively can have. The age difference indicated in the scene is an interesting characterizational aspect with which to experiment.

A: Ever since I was about four years old, I remember my family going to the ocean for the month of August. My father would always take the whole month off—he ran his own business, so he could do whatever he wanted—and we would go off to a rented cottage on St. Simon's Island. It was expensive, I think, and we were certainly never rich, but both my father and mother agreed that it was absolutely essential to the health of the family that we do it. My mother always said that it was better than a marriage counselor. Or did I say that, later on? I don't think there were such things as marriage counselors when I was a kid. Anyway, they would load us into the old '39 Ford station wagon—you know the kind with the real wood on the sides—and off we'd go. Well, let me tell you, it was wonderful. We always had the same cottage, right on the sand, the wood so weathered that it was hard to tell where the front porch ended and the beach began. They were the same color. Of course, the sand tracked into the house made the distinction between porch floor and beach even fuzzier. And my mother never fussed about bringing sand into the house. She was a demon housekeeper during the other eleven months of the year, but during August she was just relaxed. Whatever we did was fine. Of course, we knew better than to really mess up the house. We were careful. But she pretty much let us have our way. About every ten days or so she'd sweep the house out and wash five or six loads of clothes in the old Maytag on the back porch. No dryer, of course, so there'd be these long clotheslines stretched out back, bathing suits and towels and sheets snapping back and forth in the wind. There was always a pretty good breeze coming in from the Atlantic. That was one of the nice things about the island. The wind kept the mosquitoes and the sand flies down to a minimum. It was great. And, oh my, I remember the food. I'll probably never be able to eat like that again. Hot dogs cooked on sticks over a driftwood fire. Clams fried on the old gas stove and dumped right onto your plate from the frying pan, with a pile of potatoes beside them. Fresh corn on the cob. Oh, it was good. And I certainly have never slept more soundly than I did on that thin mattress stretched over those squeaky springs. The fresh breeze, the sound of the waves crashing on the beach. Youth. Slept like the dead, then woke up ready to go. Spent the whole day on the beach, running back to grab a peanut butter and jelly sandwich at noon. Turned brown as a berry by the end of the month. Always hated to go home. Oh, those August days were probably the best days of my life . . .

B: You have to look ahead, though. You know that. I think one of the greatest dangers of getting old is living too much in the past. I know you don't, of course. I really enjoyed hearing about those August days. But you have a lot to live for right now, you know? You have a good job still, and you certainly have a lot of people around you that love you and want to be with you whenever you want to be with them. So I just hope you don't dwell on the things that have gone too much. Although I guess I do the same thing to a certain extent, but in the other direction. I think about what my life is going to be like in ten years or so, and that becomes my favorite daydream. A fantasy. I'm afraid it's rather an obsession. And it involves the ocean, too, as a matter of fact. I think the thing I want most to do is to have a house on a rocky point somewhere along the Oregon coast. Maybe around Gold Beach . . . somewhere in there. I could almost drive you to the spot right now. There's a place where there's a narrow spit of land that goes out—directly west—right into the ocean for about two hundred yards. And right at the end there's a rock outcropping that completely shields the last quarter acre from view. That last quarter acre drops down about fifty feet, too, but it's still more than a hundred feet down to the water. Anyway, that's where I want to build my house. Right out of the stone that's lying around everywhere. I'd like to do it myself if I could, although I know, realistically, that I'd need some help along the way. But I bet I could do most of it myself. I see myself pitching a tent and living in it while I build one room, then gradually adding on to it as time went by. Maybe in ten years I'd have something really wonderful. I see this enormous room with a huge stone fireplace set into a wall of glass. And right out there is the ocean, the sound of big waves breaking on the rocks below. I'm telling you, I can hear those waves and feel the heat of that fire right now. If I can't go to sleep at night—and there are more and more of those nights—all I usually have to do is start visualizing myself sitting in that room just at sunset . . . watching the sun going down over the water and feeling that warm fire and listening to Mozart . . . usually sends me right off, and I have good dreams, too. Of course, I suppose that living in the future is as bad as living in the past. But I ration myself. I don't let myself build that dream castle too often. I know it can become an obsession and I know that's bad.

A: Everybody has to have dreams.

B: But not obsessions.

A: Fantasies are bad?

B: Not necessarily.

A: No.

B: Just habit-forming . . .

Scene 37

• •

Here is the opposite of the preceding scene. The lines are so short in this scene that the pace moves very, very fast. Yet there are plenty of places where judicious pauses can be inserted. Experiment with how fast pace can become and still be *fully* motivated. There is also a good deal of latitude in choosing line readings, particularly in lines that have frequently repeated words in them. Find variety for these repetitious words and phrases. Find—from nearly infinite possibilities—what motivates the transition in the last two lines.

A: There!

B: Where?

A: See?

B: No.

A: Look up.

B: I can't.

A: Why not?

B: My neck.

A: What's wrong?

B: It's stiff.

A: From what?

B: Looking up.

A: Let's rest.

B: Okay.

A: Over here.

B: There's ants.

A: Here, then.

B: Too wet.

A: Okay, where?

B: Well . . .

A: Here.

B: No.

A: Yes.

B: Okay.

A: Nice day.

B: Yes.

A: You tired?

B: No.

A: I am.

B: I'm not.

A: Okay, fine.

B: Don't whine.

A: I'm not.

B: Oh, yes.

A: No.

B: Okay, fine.

A: See any?

B: None.

A: Ever have?

B: Sure.

A: When?

B: Last year.

A: Right. Where?

B: Right here.

A: No.

B: Oh, yes.

A: Right here?

B: Very spot.

A: Unbelievable.

B: True.

A: Big ones?

B: Pretty big.

A: Fierce?

B: Relatively.

A: Get pictures?

B: A few.

A: Got any?

B: Here?

A: Uh-huh.

B: No.

A: Too bad.

B: Yeah.

A: None today.

B: No.

A: Early yet.

B: Uh-huh.

A: Still might.

B: Sure.

A: Time flies.

B: Not really.

A: Sometimes.

B: Depends.

A: On what?

B: Well . . .

A: Yes?

B: On what's . . .

A: Yes?

B: Happening.

A: Granted.

B: So . . .

A: Yes?

B: Want to play?

A: Well . . .

B: Around?

A: Sure.

B: Great!

——————————— • • • ———————————

Scenes for Three Actors

SCENE 38

• •

This scene provides the same sort of exercise in dovetailing and overlapping that Scene 28 does, but this time for three actors. You'll find that the presence of the third character complicates the problem considerably. For instance, because the length of time that an actor must motivate a pause before completing the thought is much longer, the subtext must be even more solidly based. The rhythm of the scene being quite fast and complex, the individual trains of thought must be clearly delineated.

A: Sit still now and don't be . . .

B: This is the most uncomfortable . . .

C: When do we eat? I'm . . .

A: Don't be so restless.

B: . . . seat I've ever felt. I'm . . .

C: . . . starved. You have anything . . .

A: No.

C: . . . to eat?

B: No what?

A: Just no. I'm not going to be led into this . . .

C: A candy bar or anything?

A: . . . conversation. I've said everything I have . . .

B: What conversation? What are you . . .

A: . . . to say on this topic.

B: . . . talking about?

C: What topic? Are we going to . . .

A: You know what topic. Both of you. Every time we . . .

C: . . . have any food anytime soon?

B: Oh, don't start. You're always blaming . . .

A: Every time we go someplace it's always the same . . .

B: . . . us for everything that goes wrong.

A: . . . story.

C: Oh, look. There's that woman we saw before. You know . . .

B: Where?

A: Oh, please.

C: . . . the one with the patch over one eye.

B: Oh, yeah. What do you suppose . . .

C: Looks mysterious.

B: . . . it's for?

A: Probably just for effect.

B: You think so?

A: Sure.

B: That's pretty . . .

C: No, I think she . . .

B: . . . cynical.

A: Oh?

C: . . . had an operation. Or . . .

B: Absolutely.

C: . . . something.

A: You want me to ask her?

C: Poor thing.

B: No, I do not.

A: I will.

B: I know you would. It's just the . . .

A: Just to show you.

B: . . . sort of thing you'd do.

C: Here we go again.

A: I was just kidding . . .

C: No, you weren't.

B: We've seen it before, that kind of behavior.

A: Never!

B: Yes. On many an . . .

C: Will you two please be quiet?

B: . . . occasion.

A: Honestly, you are so . . .

C: I can't stand this . . .

A: . . . bad tempered.

C: . . . constant fighting.

B: I am not. You are simply . . .

C: It's . . .

B: . . . incredibly oversensitive.

C: . . . debilitating.

A: I am not.

B: What did you say?

A: I am not.

B: No, not you.

C: Me?

B: Yes.

C: When?

B: Just now.

A: Debilitating.

B: Yes, that's right.

C: I said that?

A: Yes, you did.

C: So?

B: It sounded so odd.

C: It did not.

A: It did.

B: I thought so . . .

A: Very . . .

B: . . . didn't you?

A: . . . strange.

C: Why?

A: Well . . .

B: Unlikely. Coming from . . .

A: . . . just not like you. Not at . . .

B: . . . you.

C: You must think my . . .

A: . . . all like you.

C: . . . vocabulary is . . .

B: Pretentious, even. Like . . .

C: . . . pretty limited.

B: . . . something you'd just looked up.

A: Yes. In the . . .

C: Oh . . .

B: . . . dictionary.

C: . . . shut up.

SCENE 39

• •

The lengthy, formal speeches in this scene lend themselves, of course, to a pace that is slower than usual. But this slow pace (as well as the rather bookish quality of the speeches) presents two problems: one, that of making the dialogue seem like real speech rather than "speech making"; and, two, that of keeping the rhythm of the scene from becoming overdeliberate and artificial. Find subtextual solutions—probably based in the antagonism of two of the characters for the third—that will allow for developing a variety of characters. This will tend to move the scene along in ways that will make it more various and therefore much more interesting.

A: I have to say something.

B: See this?

C: Yes.

B: What does it look like to you?

C: I'm not sure.

A: I really have to tell you two something.

B: It's not in the book?

C: No?

B: No.

A: I feel very left out. Everything you two do is directed toward each other and I feel very isolated. Had you realized that?

B: Of course, not everything has to be in the book.

C: No, but most things are.

A: Did you know that?

B: Excuse me?

C: What did you say?

A: That you ignore me.

B: Oh, surely not.

C: Do we?

B: You're imagining things.

C: Yes.

A: No, listen, right from the beginning you two formed your own little world and I had absolutely no part in it. Everything that you do—both of you—is motivated by some interest that one of you has, and those interests never seem to have anything to do with anything that I'm interested in. It's very hard on me, to tell you the truth. I feel very shut out.

C: How extraordinary.

B: Really.

A: So I think we should talk about it. I do believe in communication, you know. I mean, I believe that if there is a problem in a group that the only really effective solution to that problem is communication, talking it out. So do you suppose we could just stop and sit down and communicate with each other about this?

C: You don't think these things just have a way of working themselves out? Do we have to go into deep analysis about it?

B: Yes. About every little thing?

C: I mean, after a while people become paranoid about the smallest things and I don't think that's healthy. I wonder if that doesn't lead us into a kind of neurotic sensibility.

A: See, it's not such a little thing to me.

B: I couldn't agree with you more.

A: Well, good, maybe we can . . .

B: No, not you. I agree that overanalysis makes people neurotic and that things should be just left alone to develop.

C: Then there's the jargon you use . . .

B: Oh, yes. I mean, if one more person tells me they want to communicate with me, I think I'll throw something big and heavy at them.

C: Exactly.

B: Doesn't it make you self-conscious? Aren't you the least little bit aware of the fact that some of these words and phrases are overused to the point of imbecility? They don't even mean what they're supposed to mean, usually. Why don't you just say "talk" instead of "communicate"?

A: Well, I for one think you two are probably the least communicative people I know.

C: There you go again.

A: Neither of you ever goes into a caring mode.

B: Jargon again.

A: Someday you may find yourself in a situation where you really do want to reach out to another human being and you're going to find that there isn't anyone there to reach out to. You'll have chased everyone away.

B: But that's the point, I think. I do believe that people are going to be friends with the people they have the most in common with.

C: Yeah. And, if I may say so, you seem to spend a lot of time trying to force yourself on other people, and maybe you should spend that energy getting to know yourself a little better. If you knew yourself better, you might find other people who related to you in a more intimate way.

A: I think that's very negative.

C: I don't mean we can't be associates, even friends, but there are degrees in relationships. And you're trying to push for a deeper intimacy than is ever likely to be possible.

B: I think that's true. It is irritating, you know, having someone constantly nagging at you to include them.

A: I apologize if I've been nagging . . . though I don't think I have. I simply presumed that, since we spent a fair amount of time together, that we were friends. Since that isn't the case, apparently, I think it would be much better if we just parted company.

B: You know, I have a younger brother who used to do this same kind of thing to me all the time. He wanted to be with me and my friends and, to be honest, we simply didn't want him there all the time. You know how that can be?

C: Absolutely. Of course, the age difference will prompt a circumstance like that, won't it?

B: Oh, of course.

A: Well, good-bye . . .

B: It seems to crop up over and over again in the most unexpected circumstances, doesn't it? This paranoia? For instance, you never expect to find it in such an environment as this, do you?

C: Certainly not.

A: I'll see you around, I guess . . .

B: The older one gets, the more one must be prepared for the unexpected, though. Not a day goes by that I'm not ready for something challenging to just drop out of the sky.

A: So long . . .

B: May I have the book for a moment? There's something I want to check.

C: Of course. Where would you like to eat this evening? I'm in the mood for Italian, I think. Or would you prefer Chinese?

B: Either's fine with me.

A: Good luck . . .

SCENE 40

• •

Here again is a scene involving a physical activity that affects pace and rhythm. With three characters, the activity itself becomes more complicated, and the pace varies even more. Toward the middle of the scene, the characters obviously perform the activity on an automatic level, which allows them to speak at different rates while still maintaining the separate rhythm dictated by the work they are doing. Once again, the activity offers a chance to exercise creative sense memory.

A: Find the end of that . . .

B: I'm doing the best I can.

C: Hold that up. Quick, quick!

B: Get it in there, get it in there!

A: All right now, be ready . . .

C: Stop!

A: What's the matter?

C: We're never going to get this done if you don't . . .

B: What?

C: Nobody's concentrating.

A: I am.

B: Me, too.

C: Well, let's try again . . . ready?

A: Yes.

B: Right.

C: Right. Now, then, one . . . two . . . three . . .

A: Steady . . .

B: Easy . . .

C: Good. Now push it right along over . . .

A: Is that supposed to . . .

B: Yes. Keep going . . .

A: Catch that . . .

B: I've got it . . . now . . .

C: Right down the middle.

A: Okay, here we go: push . . . one . . . two . . . three . . .

B: Pull . . . one . . . two . . . three . . .

C: Next . . . lift . . . center . . .

A: Push . . . one . . . two . . . three . . .

B: Pull . . . one . . . two . . . three . . .

C: Next . . . lift . . . center . . .

A: Now we got the rhythm. Keep it going . . .

B: Right. Two . . . three . . .

C: Next . . . good.

A: Push . . . how long do you think this is . . .

B: Pull . . . one . . . two . . .

C: Not too long . . .

A: Getting easier now.

B: You think it's worth it?

C: You want an ethical discussion in the middle of . . . watch out!

A: Push! One, two, three . . .

B: Can't break the rhythm.

C: I know. All right now.

A: Push . . . and it is worth it.

B: Will be.

C: Absolutely. Next . . .

B: You two think you can handle it for a minute or two?

C: Yes. Let off . . .

A: Push . . .

B: Whew, I've just about had it. Got to rest for a minute or two. You sure you're all right?

A: Yeah. It's easy, now.

C: Just keep the rhythm.

A: It's almost like it becomes second nature, you know?

C: After a while it will be. That's what they say, anyhow. Look how much easier it is now, with just a little practice.

B: Exhausting, though.

A: I'm not so tired.

B: Oh, really?

A: I didn't mean . . .

B: I know, I know. Just watch it.

C: Pull. One . . . two . . . three . . .

A: Next. Lift . . . center . . .

C: Push. One . . . two . . . three . . .

A: Now we're back on track.

B: Good work.

C: Going smoothly.

A: When we get through here, we've got to be sure that everything is cleaned up and put back in good order.

B: Absolutely. We want them to be very willing to lend us this equipment another time, right?

C: You bet. Say, you want to take over here for a while?

B: Sure . . . okay, when . . .

C: Now. Go!

B: Next. Lift . . . center . . .

A: Push. One . . . two . . . three . . .

C: Steady, now.

A: I'm next to take a break.

B: I thought you weren't tired.

A: I am now.

C: What are we going to do after that?

B: I think we should go somewhere and relax.

A: I'm for that.

C: Anybody hungry?

A: Me. I am.

B: Me, too.

C: Well, then, let's go get something to eat and then maybe watch a movie.

A: Sounds good.

B: Absolutely.

C: Got to finish this first, though.

A: Let's all get together for the final push.

C: I'm in.

A: Push. One . . . two . . . three . . .

B: Pull. One . . . two . . . three . . .

C: Next. Lift . . . center.

Glossary

The following terms are used throughout *The Actor's Scenebook*. Each of them is an acting vocabulary term currently applied in beginning and intermediate acting classes in most American universities. The definitions, while corresponding to generally accepted notions, are those of the author.

Action:	Mental, physical, or emotional activity, motivated by a textual or subtextual source, that moves the character along the rhythmic build toward the objective of the scene.
Body gesture:	A gesture in which the hands and arms relate directly to the rest of the body. The body gesture can express action but is most often used when the body is at rest: folded arms, hands on hips, hands in pockets, and so forth.
Body stance:	The way in which the body relates to the surface on which it is standing, sitting, or lying. Generally speaking, a relaxed, solid stance is the basis for all gesture and movement.
Build:	The increasing emotional intensity of a scene.

Choice: Any of a variety of decisions the actor must make regarding characterization: motivation, biographical information, line reading, rhythm, actions, and so forth.

Character analysis: A written statement of the life of the character as perceived by the actor and based on textual sources. This analysis often includes a biography, a psychological analysis, physical description, individual motivations, and other such matters, which aid the actor in making choices. Most often, actors and directors collaborate on ideas relating to character analysis.

Character biography: A written statement of the entire life of a character as perceived by the actor. Character biographies are, of course, drawn from the text but may sometimes be extended to a time before the play begins to the birth of the character or to a time after the play ends to the character's death. In such cases, the actor's projections of the origin and destiny of the character are based on the text or on valid decisions made by the actor and the director.

Characterization: The incarnation of the textual persona into the mind and body of the actor.

Circle of concentration: Projected circle of awareness into which the actor focuses his or her attention. Circles of concentration include a "personal" circle expressing the focus area a character projects when alone or in deep thought; a "shared" circle, which might include the entire acting area, including another actor or actors; and an "infinite" circle, in which a character projects thoughts and focus into memory or fantasy or extended physical space.

Commenting: Performing external actions without internal motivation, usually to elicit a specific response from the audience. Also called **indicating**.

Conflict: The opposing forces in the scene against which the character of the play or scene operates.

Cue: Words or physical circumstances that signal to the actor when it is time to speak or perform an action. Usually these occur at the end of the preceding line of dialogue, but they may include a variety of stimuli such as sound, lighting effects, other physical actions, or even individual internal processes.

Dovetailing: Beginning to speak before the preceding speech is completed, often in fast-paced situations, also called "telescoping." *See also* **interrupt**.

Emotion memory: The ability to recall a specific emotional response from the actor's life and apply it to the emotional circumstances of the character. Also called "affective memory."

Environment: The physical surroundings of the scene. Often more than a building or structure, environment may include weather and other climatic influences, terrain, noise, and so forth.

Filled pause: Pause in which silent time is occupied by a specific train of character thought. This train of thought must be sustained by the actor in objective time and is the basis of all timing, comic or otherwise.

Hand/arm gesture: Employment of the hands and/or arms away from the body in order to describe or emphasize objects, events, thoughts, or conditions.

Indicating: *See* **commenting**.

Interrupt: A specific kind of **dovetailing** in which, usually out of peremptory emotion, a character begins to speak before the preceding character has finished speaking.

Line reading: The rhythms, stresses, and motivations the actor applies to the textual line in its spoken delivery.

Listening: Part of the **present-tense acting** process in which the actor listens as the character, hearing the other lines as if for the first time.

Motivation: The underlying emotional or psychological reason for a character's speech and/or action.

Motivational unit: The demarcation of motivation into sections defined by a character's changing the direction in which he or she proceeds toward an objective. Defining these sections assists in determining overall **motivation** and in plotting the rhythm and build of a scene.

Objective: The purpose a character is trying to achieve at any time in the development of the scene.

Obstacle: An event or emotional development that works at cross-purposes to the obtaining of the objective. Obstacles often create conflict.

Pace: The overall rhythm of a scene or play, primarily dependent on the length of pauses.

Peak: The moment of greatest emotional intensity in a scene.

Phrasing: The division of a speech into cohesive spoken units as dictated by intellectual and emotional sense. These units are divided by very brief, sometimes almost imperceptible, diacritical pauses.

Present-tense acting: The process of the actor's thought and response occurring at the same time as the character's.

Rate: The speed at which an actor speaks the words of his or her individual speeches.

Reality level: How closely an actor's performance relates to and reflects the real world.

Rhythm: The dynamics of a scene's progression as it relates to build, pace, and rate.

Sense memory: The ability to recall a physical sensation and apply it to a theatrical situation in which the actual physical stimulation producing the sensation is absent. Reacting to a "pulled" punch as if one had been squarely hit is an example of the application of sense memory.

Spine: The "through-line" of a character's progress in a scene. Spine includes matters of subtextual motivation of actions in pursuit of an objective, the dynamic of rhythm (pace and rate), and the fluctuation of energy.

Subtext: The psychological and emotional meanings and motivations that form the basis of the text. Explains why and in what context a character speaks and acts.

Subverbal: Vocal sound that is not framed in words. Moans, cries, screams, grunts, and stammers are examples. Frequently not part of the written text, such subverbals can add to the effectiveness and reality of the actor's vocal delivery if used judiciously.

Superobjective: The statement of the overall goal or objective of a play or scene, the superobjective provides the through-line of motivation for individual as well as group action.

Telescoping: *See* **dovetailing**.

Topping: The geometric increase of vocal intensity and energy between two or more characters in a scene.

Trail-off: Incomplete ending of a speech in which the character is not interrupted but is unable, for various reasons, to finish the thought.

Transition: Thought pattern that takes a character from one motivational unit to another.

Vocal energy: The application of various levels of emotional intensity to the spoken word. Vocal energy is a primary tool of individual and group build. Vocal energy may also be expressed onomatopoetically, giving emotional color to certain words.

Vocal projection: The emotional and physical focusing and placement of the voice so as to be clearly heard by the audience.